The CIA's Style Manual for Intelligence Publications

The CIA's Style Manual for Intelligence Publications

GOVERNMENT REPRINTS PRESS
An imprint of
Ross & Perry, Inc.
Washington, D.C.

No claim to U.S. government work contained throughout this book.

Protected under the Berne Convention. Published 2001

Printed in The United States of America
Ross & Perry, Inc. Publishers
717 Second St., N.E., Suite 200
Washington, D.C. 20002
(202) 675-8300

SAN 253-8555

Government Reprints Press Edition 2001
Government Reprints Press is an Imprint of Ross & Perry, Inc.

Library of Congress Control Number: 2001091373

http://www.GPO.reprints.com

ISBN 1-931641-02-1

Preface

This manual provides guidance for the writing style in the Central Intelligence Agency. It has been alphabetized and indexed to enable users to find specific subjects quickly.

The mission statement from Tradecraft 2000 is, "Intelligence analysis is the process of providing objective and effective support to help US policymakers, by means of information and assessments on events overseas, to carry out their mission of formulating and implementing national security policy." When that intelligence is written, keep these concepts in mind:

- Evaluate the paper from the intended policymaker's point of view.
- Switch your focus from whether something will happen to how it could happen.
- Be aware of your reading audience. Reserve technical language for technical readers.
- Do not stray from the subject.
- Keep the language crisp.
- Keep sentences and paragraphs short, and vary the structure of both.
- Use the active voice and avoid streams of polysyllables and prepositional phrases.
- Be sure that subject and verb agree in number.
- Be sure that every pronoun has a clearly identifiable antecedent and that the two agree in number and gender.
- Use adjectives, adverbs, and figures of speech sparingly. Make sure they are properly placed to avoid confusion over which noun or verb is modified.
- Watch word breaks.
- Be objective.

Note that all examples in the General Rules section are in italics. If a word or phrase is regularly italics, it is reversed in the example.

The following abbreviations appear in our list of compound words/spelling:

adj (adjective)

adv (adverb)

ant (antonym)

cf (combining form)

comp (computer term)

n (noun or modified noun)

pl (plural)

pred (predicate)

pref (prefix)

prep (preposition)

sing (singular)

suf (suffix)

syn (synonym)

um (unit modifier)

v (verb or modified verb)

The abbreviations are sometimes used to indicate that the compound is spelled as shown only for a specified function. For example, the entry *low-key (adj)* signifies that the compound adjective (but not the noun) is always hyphenated, even in a predicate position.

Examples
- *He has a low-key approach.* (compound adjective)
- *His approach was low-key.* (predicate adjective)
- *His approach was kept in a low key.* (noun)

The listing *fire-resistant (um)* means that the compound is so spelled only as a unit modifier preceeding the word modified and not as a predicate adjective.

Examples:
- *fire-resistant material*
- *the material is fire resistant*

Bibliography

AG Style Guide, CIC, 1995.

The American Heritage Dictionary of the English Language, William Morris, ed., Boston, Houghton Mifflin Co., 1976.

A Style Manual for NPIC Products, G&PD-050/93, October 1993.

Cormier, Robin A., *Error-Free Writing: A Lifetime Guide to Flawless Business Writing*, Prentice-Hall, Inc., Englewood Cliffs, NJ, 1995.

FBIS Editorial Handbook, Foreign Broadcast Information Service, March 1993.

Hodges, John C., Whitten, Mary E., *Harbrace College Handbook*, Harcourt Brace Jovanovich, Inc., 1984.

Notes on Analytic Tradecraft, Product Evaluation Staff, Notes 1-4, 1995.

Pfaffenberger, Bryan, *Que's 1996 Computer and Internet Dictionary*, 6th edition, Que Corporation, September 1995.

Smith, Peggi, *Proofreading Manual and Reference Guide*, Editorial Experts, Inc., Alexandria, VA, 1981.

Style Manual & Writers Guide for Intelligence Publications, Fifth Edition, October 1996.

United States Government Printing Office, *Style Manual*, Washington, 1984.

Webster's Ninth New Collegiate Dictionary, Springfield, MA, Merriam-Webster, Inc., 1986 (based on *Merriam's Unabridged Webster's Third New International Dictionary*, 1961).

Contents

General Rules

abbreviations
In CIA usage, periods are usually omitted in all but a few categories of abbreviations, such as academic degrees (*Ph.D.*, *B.A.*), and terms such as *a.k.a.*, export/import terms (*f.o.b.*, *c.i.f.*), and ranks or titles (*Gen.*, *Prof.*, *Dr.*).

Change e.g. to *for example*, i.e. to *that is*, and etc. to *and so forth*.

Always abbreviate the following.

Examples

Mr.	*Dr.*	*Jr.*
Mrs.	*Esq.*	*Sr.*
Ms.		

Never abbreviate the following.

Examples

President	*Commodore*
Senator	*Commandant*
Representative	

First Reference
An organization, group, international agreement, unit of measure, weapon system, or the like that is referred to throughout a report is abbreviated after it is spelled out at the first reference, often (but not always) with its abbreviation following it in parentheses.

Examples
- *Nuclear Non-Proliferation Treaty (NPT)*
- *nautical mile (nm)*
- *multiple reentry vehicles (MRVs)*
- *airborne warning and control system (AWACS)*

If the first use of the abbreviation closely follows the spelled-out name or term and the connection between the two is clear, the parenthetical insertion should be omitted.

Examples
- *As a representative of a less developed country, the delegate purported to speak for all LDCs.*
- *The newer models, with a range of 500 nautical miles, are replacing the 400-nm versions now widely deployed.*

This alternate approach to the first-reference rule is particularly applicable to long country names that, because of repeated mention, need to be abbreviated after the first reference.

Subsequent References
In long reports, repeat the full designation every so often without respecifying the abbreviation, but continue thereafter to use the abbreviation.

Explanation Following
Sometimes it is appropriate to give an abbreviation first, with the full title or other identification in parentheses, or set off by commas, immediately afterward.

Examples
- *WHO (World Health Organization)*
- *YPF, the Argentine petroleum monopoly, . . .*

Incomplete or Possessive References
Avoid wording that would put an abbreviation immediately after an incomplete or possessive form of the name abbreviated.

Examples
- *the platform of the Liberal Democratic Party (LDP)* or *the Liberal Democratic Party (LDP) platform* (not the Liberal Democratic [LDP] platform*)*
- *the ban under the Nuclear Non-Proliferation Treaty (NPT)* (not the Nuclear Non-Proliferation Treaty's [NPT] ban)

Plural Forms
If the logical place to spell out an abbreviation comes when the term is plural, the abbreviation also must be in the plural form, even though the singular may be used thereafter.

Example
- *multiple independently targetable reentry vehicles (MIRVs)*

Unit of Measure
An abbreviation of a unit of measure has neither a period nor a plural form (*1 km, 2 km*). Upper and lower case have different meanings (see page 119).

Well-Known Abbreviations
Some abbreviations are widely recognized and need no explanation. Even these, however, should be spelled out if the context suggests a need to do so or if there is any doubt about clarity.

Examples

ABM	(antiballistic missile)	km	(kilometer)
ANC	(African National Congress)	LDC	(less developed country)
APEC	(Asia Pacific Economic Cooperation)	MIRV	(multiple independently targetable reentry vehicle)
ASEAN	(Association of Southeast Asian Nations)	MITI	(Japanese Ministry of International Trade and Industry)
AWACS	(airborne warning and control system)	NAFTA	(North American Free Trade Agreement)
BW	(biological warfare)	NATO	(North Atlantic Treaty Organization)
CFE	(Conventional Forces in Europe)	OAS	(Organization of American States)
CIA	(Central Intelligence Agency)	OAU	(Organization of African Unity)
CW	(chemical warfare)	OECD	(Organization for Economic Cooperation and Development)
DIA	(Defense Intelligence Agency)	OPEC	(Organization of Petroleum Exporting Countries)
DoD	(Department of Defense)	PLO	(Palestine Liberation Organization)
EU	(European Union)	R&D	(research and development)
FY	(fiscal year)	S&T	(science and technology)
GATT	(General Agreement on Tariffs and Trade)	SALT	(strategic arms limitation talks)
GDP	(gross domestic product)	SAM	(surface-to-air missile)
GNP	(gross national product)	SLBM	(submarine-launched ballistic missile)
IAEA	(International Atomic Energy Agency)	START	(strategic arms reduction talks)
ICBM	(intercontinental ballistic missile)	UK	(United Kingdom)
IMF	(International Monetary Fund)	UN	(United Nations)
IRBM	(intermediate-range ballistic missile)	US	(United States) (see page 121)
kg	(kilogram)	WHO	(World Health Organization)
KGB	(former Russian State Security Committee)	WTO	(World Trade Organization)

Military Ranks

These abbreviations for the most commonly used terms for military ranks—some only in non-US services—reflect the usage of the US Department of Defense and, for Russian ranks, that of OSS/KPG/Leadership Production Unit. The abbreviations are used only when they precede proper names, preferably full names. In general usage the ranks are spelled out in lowercase.

Examples

Adm.	admiral
Army Gen.	army general

Brig.	*brigadier*
Brig. Gen.	*brigadier general*
Capt.	*captain*
Capt. 1st Rank	*captain first rank*
Capt. 2nd Rank	*captain second rank*
CWO	*chief warrant officer*
Col.	*colonel*
Col. Gen.	*colonel general*
Cdr.	*commander*
Cpl.	*corporal*
Ens.	*ensign*
1st Lt.	*first lieutenant*
Flt. Adm.	*fleet admiral*
Gen.	*general*
Lt.	*lieutenant*
Lt. Col.	*lieutenant colonel*
Lt. Cdr.	*lieutenant commander*
Lt. Gen.	*lieutenant general*
Lt. (jg)	*lieutenant junior grade*
Maj.	*major*
Maj. Gen.	*major general*
Mar.	*marshal*
Pvt.	*private*
Rear Adm.	*rear admiral*
Ret.	*retired*
2nd Lt.	*second lieutenant*
Sgt.	*sergeant*
Vice Adm.	*vice admiral*
WO	*warrant officer*

Ambiguous Abbreviations

Do not use without explanation (and, if possible, avoid altogether) an abbreviation that can be construed in more than a single meaning. *NA*, for example, has been used in tables to mean "not available" as well as "not applicable." Current practice is to use NA to mean only "not available." The absence of an entry should mean "not applicable."

aboard, on board   *Aboard* can be an adjective (*the crew is aboard*), an adverb (*they went aboard*), or a preposition (*they are aboard the ship*). The prepositional phrase *on board* can be used adjectivally (*they are on board*) or adverbially (*they went on board*) but preferably not prepositionally—avoid *on board the ship*.

about, estimated	*About*, in the sense of approximately, and its counterpart *estimated* are useless when a figure is stated precisely.

absolutes	Some adjectives have no comparative or superlative modifiers.

Examples

eternal	*maximum*
extreme	*minimum*
fatal	*perfect*
full	*unique*
incessant	*universal*

academic degrees	Academic degrees in general terms are in lowercase when spelled out: *doctor of philosophy, doctorate, master of arts, master's degree, bachelor of arts, bachelor's degree.* But capitalize when the full name of the degree is given or when it follows a person's name.

Examples

- *Bachelor of Arts in Business Administration*
- *Master of Science in Biology*
- *Jane Smyth, Doctor of Philosophy*

For plural abbreviations, *Ph.D.'s; M.A.'s; B.A.'s.*

acronyms	Explain them as you would any other abbreviation. But be aware that acronyms do not always seem to follow conventions about capitalization or other matters (*Aramco, NATO, agitprop*). Usually, when an acronym is made up solely from the first letter of the major words in the expanded form, render the acronym in all capitals (*North Atlantic Treaty Organization*, or *NATO*).

We write *comsat* when speaking generally of a communications satellite, but *Comsat* in reference to the corporation. The term *Landsat* should refer only to the US Earth resources satellite, but *landsat* might be used in a less specific reference.

active vs. passive voice	In formal writing the active voice is usually preferred. *Lifeguards clear beaches when forecasters predict storms.* Only if your focus is beach clearing rather than lifeguards would the passive voice be preferred. *The beaches are cleared when storms are forecast.*

adverbs	Modify a verb, an adjective, or another adverb. They should be placed near the words they modify. When an adverb is placed within a verb it should regularly follow the first auxiliary, not precede it.

Example
• *The Prime Minister has finally announced his decision.*

adverse, averse	They sound alike and both express opposition, but their meanings are not the same. *Adverse* applies to something working against a person or program.

Example
• *adverse weather conditions*

Averse applies to a person who is against something.

Example
• *He is averse to traveling abroad.*

affect, effect	*Affect*, as a verb, means to influence, to produce an effect upon.

Example
• *The blow on the head affected John's vision.*

Effect, as a verb, means to bring about.

Example
• *The assailant effected a change in John's vision by striking him on the head.*

Effect can be used as a noun.

Example
• *The effect of the blow on John's head was blurred vision.*

affinity	Describes a reciprocal relationship. The preposition used after *affinity* is *between*, *of*, or *with*, not for or to. *Affinity between* (or *of*) two persons or two things; *affinity with* one person or one thing.

ages	**Persons** These are expressed in figures except at the beginning of a sentence and in approximations by decades.

Examples
- *The general is almost 60 (or 60 years old, not 60 years of age).*
- *General Manley, 60 (or age 60, not aged 60), is retiring at the end of the year. (Age 60 is appropriate at the beginning of one of the short, biographic summaries known as snowflakes.)*
- *The general must be in his sixties.*
- *Five-year-olds who will reach their 6th birthday by 31 December are eligible.* (Change sentence to begin: *All 5-year-olds . . .*)

Inanimate Things
These are given according to the basic rules for numbers above and below 10.

Examples
- *The program is two years old.*
- *Those 30-year-old submarines are being scrapped.*

also

Used as a direct modifier of a negative verb—he also does not favor import quotas—is unidiomatic. Do one of three things:

1. Move the word to modify the whole sentence or clause.

Example
- *Also, he does not favor import quotas.*

2. Replace it.

Examples
- *He does not favor import quotas either.*
- *Moreover, he does not favor import quotas.*

3. Make the verb positive.

Example
- *He also opposes import quotas.*

Be sure, moreover, that *also* is intended to modify the verb directly and not some other word in the sentence; *also*, like *even* and *only*, can be a misplaced modifier.

always

Is on every occasion or forever. Be sure that you do not use always when you mean habitually or usually.

ambivalent, ambiguous

Ambivalent applies to mixed feelings, the simultaneous operation in the mind of two different and usually conflicting desires. If you wish to point out uncertainty or lack of clarity, the proper word is *ambiguous*.

American spelling	When American and British spellings of common English words differ, the American spelling is always used, even when these common words form part of a proper name usually spelled with British English.

Examples
- *Industrialization (*not Industrialisation*) Board*
- *Israel Defense (*not Defence*) Forces*
- *Labor (*not Labour*) Party*
- *Minister for Defense (*not Defence*)*
- *Programs (*not Programmes*) Chair* |
and, but, however	As connectives may be used at the beginning of a sentence when emphasis is desired.
anglicized foreign words	Many foreign words and phrases have been thoroughly anglicized (*coup d'etat, in absentia, per se*). Others are not as easily comprehended by American readers and, unless there is no equivalent English expression, should not be used (for example: ad hominem, passim). For a specific anglicized word, check the Compound Words/Spelling section.
anticipate, expect	When you *anticipate* an event, you generally make some preparation for it; when you *expect* an event, you simply await developments before acting.
apostrophe	Two functions of the *apostrophe* are to show possessive case and sometimes to create plural forms. (It is also used to indicate contractions in words such as *can't* and *it's* that are appropriate in spoken but not in formal written English.)

General Rule
The possessive form made up of an apostrophe and an *s* (*the Minister's*) is used for nouns denoting persons, and the form combining the preposition *of* and a noun object is applied to organizations or inanimate things (*a decision of the Ministry*). However, the *s* possessive is commonly used for the inanimate in expressions that indicate time (*moment's notice, year's labor*) and in other familiar phrases (*heaven's sake, heart's content*). Which possessive form to use often depends on sound or rhythm: the *s* possessive is more terse than the *of* phrase (*morning's beauty, beauty of the morning*). In some *of* phrases, idiom calls for a sort of possessive redundancy—always for a pronoun (*friend of his*), usually for a proper noun (*friend of John's*) but not necessarily (*friend of John Jones*), and optionally for a common noun (*friend of the author, friend of the author's*). |

Possessives

The possessive case of most nouns and indefinite pronouns is indicated by some combination of the apostrophe and the letter *s*.

If a word (either singular or plural) does not end in *s*, add an apostrophe and an *s* to form the possessive.

Examples

the woman's book	*the women's books*
the child's shoes	*the children's shoes*
that Thai's passport	*those Thai's passports*

If the singular of a word (or acronym or abbreviation) ends in a sibilant—*s* sound—add an apostrophe and an *s* unless the added sibilant is not present in the word's normal pronunciation; in such cases, add only the apostrophe.

Examples

Athens's	*Honduras's*
CBS's	*Juarez's troops*
Congress's	*Paris's history*
Dickens's novels	*Shays's Rebellion*
but:	
the corps' units	*Marchais' leadership*
note also:	
the Comoros' climate	*the United Arab Emirates' oil*
the Netherlands' canals	*the United States' position*
the Philippines' outer islands	

To avoid a triple sibilant, exceptions are sometimes made for significant names that already end in a double sibilant.

Examples

Jesus'	*Moses'*

If the plural of a word ends in *s*, add only the apostrophe.

Examples

the boys' team	*the Joneses' address*	*the two leaders' rift*

Remember that a gerund takes a possessive.

Examples

- *No one was happy with Charlie's taking over the firm.*
- *London announced it had no objection to Rome's taking part. (Better: London announced it would not object if Rome took part.)*

9

• *Economy was one reason for George's buying a small car. (Better: Economy was one reason George bought a small car.)*

Numerical expressions in the possessive case require an apostrophe but not a hyphen.

Examples
• *After five years' planning, the project got under way.*
• *She put 16 days' work into the project.*
• *The new regime bought several million dollars' worth of arms (but $20 million worth).*

In compounds, make only the last word possessive.

Examples
• *commander in chief's decision*
• *secretary general's speech*
• *Shah of Iran's overthrow*
• *someone else's hat*

If the compound is plural, use the *of* possessive unless the plural is formed in the final word of the compound.

Examples
• *decisions of the attorneys general*
but:
• *the general counsels' decisions*

In a combination of two or more nouns for which joint possession is to be indicated, make only the last noun possessive; if individual possession, make both or all nouns possessive.

Examples
• *Pat and Mike's get-together for lunch is scheduled for 17 March.*
• *Pat's and Mike's lunchtimes never seem to coincide.*

The possessive case is often used even though ownership is not involved.

Examples
• *five years' toil*
• *for pity's sake*
• *several million dollars' worth (but $10 million worth)*
• *a day's pay*
• *for old times' sake*
• *minutes' time*
• *two hours' work*

However, do not use the apostrophe with the possessive form of personal pronouns.

Examples

his	*ours*
hers	*yours*
*its (*do not confuse with the contraction it's [it is])	*theirs*

Other Uses

In geographic names, firm names, the names of organizations and institutions, and the titles of publications, follow the authentic form.

Examples

Barclay's Bank	*Johns Hopkins University*
Court of St. James's	*Lloyds* (bank)
Harpers Ferry	*Lloyd's* (insurance)
People's Republic	*St. Peter's Church*
Reader's Digest	

Do not use an apostrophe after names of states or countries and other organized bodies ending in *s*, or after words more descriptive than possessive, except when the plural does not end in *s*.

Examples

farmers union	*officers club*
foreign ministers meeting	*Olympic Games facilities*
General Motors plant	*teachers college*
Kansas law	*Weight Watchers meeting*
League of Nations mandate	*writers guide*

but:
• *National Organization of Women's headquarters*

also:
• *master's degree, masters' degrees*

Plurals

The apostrophe is inserted before a lowercase *s* to form the plurals of single letters and digits and of abbreviations ending with a period. It is not inserted before the *s* in the plurals of groups of letters or hyphenated letter-number combinations unless needed to enhance comprehension—for example, if the combination ends with a lowercase letter (*SS-N-3a's*). It is omitted in the plurals of groups of digits designating decades or centuries.

Examples
- *dotted i's, 7's, 8's, 180 g's (but SS-7s, SS-8s)*
- *H-Is and H-IIs (but type I's)*
- *Kresta-IIs, Delta-IIs (but Flogger B's, Bear G's, Scud B's)*
- *Pershing Ia's (but Pershing IIs)*
- *SS-N-4s (but Mod 2's; all Mods of the SS-11)*
- *the 1990s (do not confuse this with the possessive forms, such as 1992's accelerated test schedule)*
- *RVs*
- *Boeing 747s*
- *11s and 13s*
- *MiGs*
- *Ph.D.'s, M.A.'s*

To form the plurals of spelled-out numbers, of most words referred to as words, and of words already containing an apostrophe, add just *s* or *es*.

Example
- *One of Bernstein's best style books is* Dos, Don'ts & Maybes of English Usage.

---

armed forces

Use plural verb (unless abbreviated [SAF]).

---

around, approximately

Around is acceptable in approximations of time. It is not always an acceptable synonym for *approximately.*

---

as

In positive comparisons, *as* is followed by another *as.*

Example
- *She is as clever as her adversary.*

In negative comparisons, *so* may be substituted for the first *as.*

Example
- *She is not so clever as her adversary.*

---

assure, ensure, insure

Assure applies to persons (*to assure a leader of one's loyalty*). Use *ensure* to mean make certain, and save *insure* for what insurance companies do.

---

awhile, a while

Awhile is not preceded by for.

Example
- *He stayed awhile;* but *he stayed for a while.*

---

based on, due to, owing to	*Based on, due to,* and *owing to* are frequent lead-ins for dangling phrases, such as due to (or owing to) illness, the meeting was postponed. Substitute *because of* for the due to, but rephrasing would be better. Do not resort to sentences like Based on Embassy reporting, he forecast another strike. The quick fix is to say *on the basis of*, but, again, try rephrasing. Try substituting *attributable to*. Note that *because of* usually begins an adverbial phrase, *due to* always begins an adjectival one.

Examples
- *estimated* (v) *on the basis of prewar inventory*
- *an estimate* (n) *based on prewar inventory*

bemused	Confused or bewildered, not synonymous with amused.

between, among	*Between* expresses the relationship of two things. *Between* can also be used to express the relationship of three or more persons or things considered individually.

Example
- *A treaty between the three nations.*

When the relationship of three or more is vague or collective, use *among*.

biographic information	Including proper spelling of personal names, is the responsibility of OSS/KPG/Leadership Production Unit.

bits, bytes	Considered units of measure and are quantified in figures.

Examples

a 7-bit byte	*5 bytes of 7 bits each*
but:	
five 7-bit bytes	

blatant, flagrant	Both describe antisocial behavior. *Blatant*, however, implies offensive bluster, while *flagrant* implies glaring evil. A person who blunders is guilty of a *blatant* error. One who willfully violates a pledge commits a *flagrant* act.

bloc	Is usually not capitalized when standing alone, not even when modified, as in *the Likud bloc.*

Exception

• *former Soviet Bloc*

---

boats, ships

Boats, nautically speaking, are usually small craft that can be carried on a *ship*, which is a larger vessel. The exception is a submarine, which may be called either a boat or a ship.

---

both

Is restricted to two. The word is sometimes used unnecessarily in an expression like *both agree* or *both share*.

---

both . . . and

The material that follows must be in balance.

Example

• *He was deaf to both argument and entreaty.* (Not: He was both deaf to argument and entreaty.)

---

boycott, embargo

Boycott is a refusal, usually by an organized group, to buy or use a particular product or service. It is not synonymous with *embargo*, which is a legal restriction on trade.

---

brackets

Brackets are used to enclose a parenthetical word or expression within a set of parentheses.

Example

• *He is well educated (by tutors in Pittsburg [Kansas]).*

Brackets are used to set off editorial remarks within quoted material.

Example

• *The Minister stated, "The election [of 3 March] will be reexamined."*

Brackets are used to enclose numbers referring to sources listed at the end of a report. (Such usage is discouraged, however, and, if essential, should be explained in a prefatory note or footnote.)

Example

• *Adams's strong defense of that law [2] was subsequently challenged by his own son in an essay [3] published after the father's death.*

[*Sic*] is put in brackets and in italics to show that a quoted passage is precisely reproduced (including mistakes).

breach, breech	As a noun, *breach* is a violation, a gap, or a rift in a solid structure. Do not confuse it with *breech,* which is acceptable only in reference to ordnance and to human anatomy.

Exception

A fighter—military, political, or otherwise—goes "once more into the breach."

bullets	The solid circular symbols used to introduce special items set off within a column of text are called *bullets*. In this function they may be used instead of or in combination with em dashes, as in a series of indented, itemized blocks of text in which some blocks are subsets of more important ones.

The bullets for formal writing, unlike PDB ticks, are structural. There should be at least two bullets. Their purpose is to organize the presentation of detail, often quite a large amount of detail. The bullets are parallel so the reader is never far from the point being discussed.

Capitalize the first letter of all material introduced by a bullet or an em dash and end each phrase with a period or a question mark. Introduce the material with a colon at the end of the introductory sentence or phrase.

Examples:

- *This would be a primary bullet phrase (or clause).*
- *This would be another primary bullet phrase.*
  - *This would be a secondary phrase subordinate to the bullet phrase above.*
  - *This would be another secondary phrase.*
- *This would be the next primary phrase.*
  - *Phrases pertinent to this phrase then would be listed under it like this.*
  - *And this.*
- *This would be the last primary bullet phrase.*

cadre	Refers to a group or nucleus, often military, around which a larger group or organization can be formed. In Communist parlance, cadre means not just a party group, or cell, but one of its members. Use an English term if possible. Always add an *s* when the word is plural.
calculus	Should be used only in reference to mathematics or pathology, not to someone's thought processes.
capitalization	In general: "if in doubt, don't." Do not, for example, capitalize the first letters of the words explaining an uppercase abbreviation unless the term abbreviated is a proper name.

Example

- *USPS (United States Postal Service)*
- *LAN (local area network)*

Party, Church, Government

When used to mean a political organization, the word *party* is capitalized only when the organization's proper name is used. The same is true of *church* and *government*.

Examples

- *the Christian Democratic Party,* but *the party*
- *the Evangelical Church,* but *the church*
- *the Israeli Government,* or *the Government of Israel,* but *the government*

Wars

Capitalize the *W* in *October War* or *Six-Day War* because either term as a whole is a distinguishing coined name, but *1973 Middle East war* or *1967 Arab-Israeli war* is distinguishing enough without the capital *W*. Avoid Yom Kippur war. Do not uppercase the w in *Korean war*, which was "undeclared"; the same logic applies to *Vietnam war* and *Falklands war*, and a similar convention to *Iran-Iraq war* and *Gulf war*.

Holidays, Feasts, Historic Events

Names of holidays and religious feasts and the names used to designate historic or otherwise significant events are capitalized. Many of the uppercased examples in this paragraph can be said to need capitalization to give them the emphasis or prominence essential to understanding their meaning, especially when they are used out of context.

Examples

(the) New Year   *the 19th Party Conference*

D-Day	*the 23rd Party Congress*
Independence Day	*the Cold War*
Labor Day	*the Cultural Revolution*
New Year's Day	*the Depression*
Ramadan	*the Feast of the Passover*
Second World War	*the Great Leap Forward*
Veterans Day	*the Holocaust*
World War II	*the Prague Spring*
the Renaissance	

Congressional

Capitalize Congressional in any reference to the US Congress, but otherwise lowercase this and other adjectival forms of words referring to government bodies unless they are part of an official name or title: Congressional (Departmental, Ministerial) Liaison Office(r), but congressional (referring to a foreign legislature) action, parliamentary elections, departmental policy, ministerial reaction. Note also that Senator or Representative is uppercased when referring to a member of the US Congress.

Presidential

Capitalize Presidential in any reference to a past or present US President (Presidential vetoes, decisions, proclamations) but not a reference to a future one (the 1996 presidential election) or to the office generally (presidential powers under the US Constitution). Outside the US context, lowercase presidential and other adjectives referring generally to government offices unless they are part of an official name or title: Presidential (Ministerial, Vice-Presidential) Liaison Office(r), the woman designated Premier, the man elected Vice President; but presidential (referring to a non-US presidency) action, ambassadorial courtesies, prime-ministerial caliber.

---

chemical terms

The hyphen is not used in a unit modifier composed of chemical terms.

Example
- *carbon monoxide poisoning*

China, Taiwan

The full name of the People's Republic of China usually is shortened to *China*. PRC may be used. After 1 July 1997 Hong Kong will officially be called the Hong Kong Special Administrative Region. *Chinese* is the preferred adjective and refers only to the mainland.

For what we used to call Nationalist China or the Republic of China, use only *Taiwan*, both as noun and adjective. For variation *Taipei* may be used in either noun or adjective form (for example, the *officials in Taipei*, or *the Taipei authorities*), but avoid *Taiwanese* as an adjective referring to the island's administration or its officials (and do not use the word government).

The terms *Communist China* (and *Chinese Communist*) and *Nationalist China* (and *Chinese Nationalist*) or *Republic of China* should be used only in historical contexts.

---

coined names

A coined name or short form for a military, economic, political, or other grouping is capitalized.

Examples

- *the Alliance, Allied (*adjective*), and Allies in reference to NATO* (uppercasing is needed for clarity, otherwise lowercase)
- *the EU, the Community(ies)*
- *the Big Seven*
- *the Free World* (use *non-Communist world* in all but historical contexts)
- *Nonaligned Movement, Nonaligned summit*
- *the Intelligence Community*
- *the Group of 77*
- *the Gang of Four*
- *the Contras*
- *Neutral Zone*

but:

- *the Persian Gulf states, the Gulf states*
- *START Treaty*
- *the stealth bomber, stealth technology, counterstealth*
- *the occupied territories*
- *the establishment*
- *fifth column*
- *Camp David accords, Geneva accords, Helsinki accords, Amman accords, Dayton accords, Paris accords* (but *Trilateral Accords* [Ukraine])

---

collective nouns

Take a singular verb when they refer to the group as a unit.

Examples

- *My family has its traditions.*
- *The number is very small.*
- *A billion dollars is a lot of money.*
- *The majority of it was wasted.*
- *Two-thirds of this has been finished.*

Take a plural verb when they refer to individuals or parts of the group.

Examples

- *A number were absent.*
- *The majority of us are for it.*
- *Two-thirds of these have been finished.*

Options

Examples

- *Ten gallons of gas is/are expensive.*
- *A thousand bushels of grain was/were crated.*

---

colon

Final Clause or Phrase

Use a colon before a final clause or phrase that summarizes or expands preceding matter.

Examples

- *Food, clothing, fuel, and building materials: these are the critical items.* (Note one space after the colon.)
- *The delegation visited four American cities: Baltimore, Chicago, San Antonio, and Denver.*
- *Jones served in three Ministries: Economy; Communications, Power, and Industry; and Agriculture.*

Two Main Clauses

Use a colon to separate two main clauses if the second amplifies or explains the first. (Otherwise, use a semicolon.)

Examples

- *Railroading is not a variety of outdoor sport: it is a service.*
- *He is well qualified to serve as Foreign Minister: he has held posts in the Ministry since 1987 and has served abroad many times.*

Titles

Use a colon to separate titles and subtitles.

Example

- *The Tragic Dynasty: A History of the Romanovs*

Ratios

Use a colon to show ratios, for which figures (not spelled-out words) are always used. But use a hyphen if the ratio is used adjectivally.

Example

- *20:1,* but *a 20-to-1 chance*

When a number following a colon begins an independent clause that you cannot recast, spell it out.

Lengthy Material

Use a colon to introduce lengthy material set off from the rest of the text by indentation. If the material set off is a quotation that is indented, no quotation marks are needed.

---

combined, joint

Referring to military exercises, mean different things: a *combined* exercise involves the forces of more than one country, a *joint* exercise involves two or more services of the same country.

---

comma

There is a general tendency to use too many commas, but omitting them is almost as common as overusing them. (One example is the comma splice, in which a comma is used instead of a semicolon or period to denote cessation rather than pause.)

The comma is used to separate two words or figures that might otherwise be misunderstood.

Examples

- *Of the total, production was the greatest single item.*
- *To his younger brother, Murray was a paragon whose every action was to be imitated.*
- *Instead of thousands, hundreds were built.*
- *In 1993, 523 units were completed. (or In 1993 about 500 units . . .)*

The comma is used to separate from each other the parts of a series of coordinate modifying words (if you can substitute *and* for the comma, the words are coordinate).

Examples

short, swift streams   *long, slender, brittle stems*

The comma is not used if the modifying words are cumulative and not coordinate (and cannot be separated by and)—that is, if one modifies another or a unit of which another is a part.

Examples

illegal drug traffic   *short tributary streams*

The comma is used to set off nonrestrictive words, phrases, or clauses.

Examples

- *The chairperson, Paul Williams, spoke last.*
- *The work was, in fact, completed.*
- *The coach, who was dismissed in 1992, was reappointed in 1993.*
- *His brother, Joseph, was appointed.* (He had only one brother.)
- *Mitchell's novel,* Gone With the Wind, *was a bestseller.* (She wrote only one novel.)
- *Actual production, however, was lower.*
- *The President, Bill Clinton, jogs.*

Whether the element is nonrestrictive, or nonessential, is determined by the intent of the sentence. Note that in the following sentences each of the elements that are nonrestrictive in the sentences above is necessary to the meaning of the sentence in which it appears. It is therefore restrictive and is not set off by commas.

Examples

- *Cochair Williams spoke last (not Cochair Johnson).*
- *The work must be completed in fact as well as in theory.*
- *The coach who was dismissed in 1992 was rehired in 1993.* (The *who* clause identifies the particular coach being discussed.)
- *His brother Joseph was appointed.* (He had more than one brother.)
- *Jones's novel* From Here to Eternity *was his biggest seller.* (He wrote several novels.)
- *President Bill Clinton jogs.*

The comma is used to set off contrasting statements in a sentence.

Example

- *Clinton, not Gore, made the decision.*

The comma is used after each element except the last—but including the next to last—within a series of three or more words, phrases, clauses, letters, or figures used with *and* or *or* (if none of the elements in the series is a phrase or clause with internal commas).

Examples

- *Copper, lead, zinc, and tin were mined.*
- *The data were collected, estimates were made, and conclusions were drawn.*
- *Complete forms A, B, and C by writing 1, 2, or 3.*

If one or more of the elements in the series is a phrase or clause with internal commas, use semicolons instead of commas between the elements, rearranging the sentence if necessary to put the series at the end. Use the semicolon before the *and* or *or*.

Example

- *The chief exports were brass, which is an alloy; platinum, which is a precious metal; and tin.* (Never: Brass, which is an alloy; platinum, which is a precious metal; and tin were the chief exports.)

The comma is used before the coordinating conjunction in a compound sentence (a sentence that contains at least two independent clauses).

Examples

- *He served in the Army until 1991, and then he went to work for the telephone company.*
- *The country imports copper, iron, and lead, but domestic tin is available.*

In a simple sentence with a compound predicate, the comma is not used before the coordinating conjunction unless needed for clarity.

Examples

- *He served in the Army until 1992 and then went to work in a bank.*
- *He went to Russia to study but decided not to stay.*

but:

- *He goes to sleep the minute he hits the mattress, and springs out of bed in the morning always eager to begin a new day.*

The comma is used to separate digits of most numbers in the thousands and unrounded millions.

Examples

- *399,243,046*
- *5,752,194* (if rounded, *5.75 million, 5.8 million,* or *6 million*)

The comma is used to separate from a main clause an introductory clause or phrase that is long or that might cause confusion without a comma.

Examples

- *Because the corporation derived much of its 1994 income from suburban outlets, it established several new ones in 1995.*

but:

- *After his defeat he retired from public life.*

The comma is used to separate a beginning participial phrase modifying the subject or an absolute phrase before the subject. Also, if it contributes to easier reading, place a comma before an opening adverbial phrase stating a year.

Examples

- *To begin with, Smith worked as an engineer.*

- *In 1986 the tragedy at Chornobyl' occurred.*
- *In 1987, Gorbachev formulated his policies of* glasnost *and* perestroyka.

Note that, whereas no comma is needed after 1986 in the above example, in the ensuing one, when the year is followed by an uppercased word, insertion of a comma aids quick comprehension—**but such a comma is optional**.

The comma is used to separate the title of a person and the name of an organization in the absence of the words *of* or *of the*.

Example

- *director, Coal Division, Ministry of Mines*

The comma is used to indicate omission of a word or words (usually a verb), unless the construction is clear enough without commas.

Example

- *In spring and fall there is hiking; in summer, sailing; in winter, skiing.*

The comma is used to separate an introductory phrase from a short direct quotation.

Example

- *He said, "Now or never."*

The comma is used to set off: a province, state, or country name from a city name; Jr. (but not III or IV) following a personal name; and Inc., Ltd., or S.A. after a corporate name. If the setting off occurs in midsentence, a comma must be used after as well as before.

Examples

- *Born in London, England, he works in the London, Ontario, area.*
- *John Jones, Jr., heads Dictionaries, Inc., and his son John Jones III runs the Georgetown branch.*

---

common basic elements

When two or more hyphenated compounds have a common basic element and this element is omitted in all but the last or first term, the hyphens are retained.

Examples

- *two- or three-year period*
- *first-, second-, and third-grade students*
- *the British- and French-produced Concorde*
- *ground- and air-launched missiles*
- *US-owned and -operated companies*

but:

- *twofold or threefold* (not two or threefold)
- *oil and gas fields,* or *oilfields and gasfields* (not oil and gasfields)
- *mid- and late 1980s (*but *mid-to-late 1980s)*
- *early or mid-1990s (*but *early-to-mid-1990s; early-to-middle 1990s)*

Use of the hyphenated prefix *mid-* in the examples shown is not incorrect, but the hyphen makes it awkward to combine *mid-* with the other, unhyphenated elements, *early* and *late.* For this reason it is recommended that *middle* rather than *mid-* be used when a combination is involved.

Examples

middle and late 1980s	*early or middle 1990s*
early and middle 1990s	*early-to-middle 1990s*

---

communications

As an adjective it usually retains the *s.* As a noun it sometimes drops the *s,* as in *sea lines of communication.*

---

comparatives, superlatives

The hyphen is usually—but not always—omitted in a two-word unit modifier in which the first word is a comparative or superlative, but, for clarity's sake, should be retained in certain three-word modifiers.

Examples

less developed countries	*worst case scenario*
but:	
higher-than-market price	*most-sought-after tickets*
lighter-than-air craft	*on-the-job training*
most-favored-nation clause	*single-most-important job*

In examples, such as *biggest bargain airline,* if the superlative applies to the bargain and not to the airline, a hyphen would be welcome after biggest.

---

compare, contrast

Compare to points out likenesses; *compare with* points out both likenesses and differences; *contrast with* points out only differences.

Examples

- *He compared his cabinet with Kennedy's.*
- *He contrasted his cabinet with Kennedy's.* (They had no similarities.)

When using *compared* as a participle, precede it with *as.*

Example

- *Production will remain at low levels as compared with the heyday of Soviet times.*

compel, impel, propel	*Compel* means to drive or urge forcefully. *Impel* is to drive or urge by moral pressure. *Propel* is to drive or urge by a force that imparts motion.

compound terms

Separate Words

One means of word combination is simply to write two words in sequence, without joining them or connecting them with a hyphen, if this formulation causes no ambiguity in sense or difficulty of comprehension.

Examples

blood pressure	*music teacher*
eye opener	*real estate*
living costs	*word combination*

Joined or Hyphenated

Often, however, words have to be joined (written solid) or connected with a hyphen to express an idea that would not be as clear if they were not so compounded.

Examples

18-year-olds	*cross-reference*	*right-of-way*
afterglow	*need-to-know*	*whitewash*
bookkeeping	*newsprint*	

Derivatives

Once formed, a compound can sprout derivatives that usually retain the hyphenated or unhyphenated (solid) form of the original.

Examples

coldbloodedness	*ill-advisedly*	*railroader*
cost-effectiveness	*in-country*	*stick-to-it-iveness*
footnoting	*praiseworthiness*	*X-rayed*

Solid Compounds

When two nouns form a compound that then has a primary accent, it is written solid, especially when the prefixed noun consists of only one syllable or when one of the elements loses its original accent.

Examples

bathroom	*bookseller*	*pipeline*
but:		
bomb bay	*coal mine*	*night shift*

The verb agrees with the compound subject closest to it.

Plurals

For the plurals of compound terms, use the plural form of the significant word or words. If there is no significant word, the plural is formed on the last word.

Combining Forms

A noun formed by combining a short verb and an adverb is usually written solid, but it is hyphenated when the solid form risks misinterpretation. The verb (v) forms of such combinations usually remain two words.

Examples

buildup (v, build up)	*giveaway (v, give away)*	*setup (v, set up)*
cut-in (v, cut in)	*run-in (v, run in)*	*tie-in (v, tie in)*

Compounds beginning with the following nouns are usually solid.

Examples

book (bookstore)	*house (housekeeping)*	*shop (shopworn)*
eye (eyeglasses)	*school (schoolteacher)*	*work (workday)*

Compounds ending in the following are usually solid when the prefixed word consists of one syllable, but not as often when the prefixed word has several syllables (*spaceborne*, but *satellite-borne*, *helicopter-borne*).

Examples

boat (rowboat)	*like (boxlike)*	*time (halftime)*
book (textbook)	*maker (steelmaker)*	*ward (homeward)*
borne (spaceborne)	*owner (homeowner)*	*way (seaway)*
bound (landbound)	*person (salesperson)*	*wide (worldwide)*
grower (applegrower)	*piece (mouthpiece)*	*wise (edgewise)*
hearted (halfhearted)	*power (airpower)*	*work (artwork)*
holder (shareholder)	*proof (blastproof)*	*worker (pieceworker)*
house (boathouse)	*room (chartroom)*	*working (woodworking)*
keeper (beekeeper)	*shop (toolshop)*	*writer (speechwriter)*
light (moonlight)	*tight (airtight)*	*yard (shipyard)*

Write solid (unhyphenated) a combination of *any*, *every*, *no*, or *some* and *body*, *thing*, or *where*; when *one* is the second element, write as two words if the meaning is a particular person or thing; to avoid mispronunciation, write *no one* as two words at all times.

Examples

anybody	*nowhere*
everything	*someone*

but:
- *Some one choice must be made, and any one of you can make it. Will no one volunteer?*

The pronouns ending in *self* and *selves* are always solid compounds.

Examples

herself	*oneself*	*themselves*
itself	*ourselves*	*yourself*

Compass Direction

Write as one word a compass direction consisting of two points, but use a hyphen after the first point when three points are combined.

Examples

northeast   *north-northeast*

Three-Word Unit Modifiers

Do not use hyphens in a three-word unit modifier in which the first word is an adverb modifying the second word.

Examples
- *unusually well preserved specimen*
- *very well defined line*
- *very high altitude resort*

exceptions:
- *very-high-frequency broadcasts*
- *very-low-frequency transmissions*
- *extremely-low-frequency communications*

But, if the first word of a three-word unit modifier modifies the other two, the hyphen is used between those two.

Examples
- *a nearly right-angle bend*
- *a formerly well-known person*
- *a virtually self-educated man*

Other Compound Words

Do not use a hyphen in a compound title denoting a single civil office or military office, but use a hyphen in a double title.

Examples

ambassador at large	*editor in chief*	*secretary-treasurer*
commander in chief	*manager-director*	*minister-counselor*

but:
under-secretaryship, under secretary   *vice-presidency, vice president*

Apart from titles, hyphens are used in some—but not all—noun compounds containing a prepositional phrase.

Examples

government-in-exile   *grant-in-aid*   *man-of-war*
but:
next of kin   *prisoner of war*   *state of the art*

Use hyphens in improvised compounds.

Examples

boardroom full of know-it-alls   *first-come-first-served basis*
bread-and-butter issue   *hard-and-fast rule*
carrot-and-stick approach   *need-to-know*
divide-and-rule   *technical know-how*

Hyphenate the verb forms of noun forms written as two words.

Examples

* *missile in flight test (to flight-test a missile)*
* *proof with blue pencils (to blue-pencil galleys)*
* *turn a cold shoulder (to cold-shoulder an idea)*

Use a hyphen to join a single capital letter to a noun or participle.

Examples

H-bomb   *T-jetty*   *X-ray*
I-beam   *T-shaped*

comprise, compose, include	*Comprise* means to contain or to consist of—*the whole comprises its parts.* *Compose* means to constitute or to make up—*the parts compose the whole.* *Comprise* is used when the reference is to all components, *include* when only some of them are mentioned. Never use comprised of.
computerese	Be aware of your reading audience and limit computer terminology in nontechnical writing.
concern	Takes different prepositions for different senses.

Examples

- *He is concerned with computers* (he is so occupied or employed).
- *He is concerned about computers* (he is worried about them).

consider, regard	*Consider*, in the sense of coming to a belief after careful deliberation, is usually not followed by *as*, but *regard*, in the same meaning, is followed by *as*.

Examples

- *He considered the vote a defeat.*
- *He regarded the vote as a defeat.*

continual, continuous, continuing	*Continual* applies to something that occurs intermittently or is repeated at intervals. *Continuous* refers to something that is uninterrupted in time or space. *Continuing* can be used in either sense.
contract	One contracts a disease.
convince, persuade	They are not interchangeable. A person is *convinced* of a need or *convinced* that a need exists after he has been *persuaded* to recognize the need.
could, may, might	*Could* should be limited to statements dealing with capability. Use *may* (past tense is *might*) when you are making judgments or predictions or indicating permission. Neither *could* nor *may* should have modifiers like conceivably and possibly.

country names

Not Abbreviated

Do not abbreviate when the country is mentioned only once or twice, or when it is mentioned in a series in which other country names are spelled out.

Abbreviated

There will be situations in which repeated reference to countries with long names calls for abbreviation. In such instances, spell out the name at the first reference and use the abbreviation, as a noun or an adjective, thereafter.

Example

- *the United Arab Emirates is . . . the UAE is . . . a UAE delegation arrived . . .*

Note that some country names, like this one (and that of our own country), are plural in construction but take singular verbs. Some country names are compounds—Trinidad and Tobago is (adjective: Trinidadian; Tobagonian); Sao Tome and Principe is (adjective: Sao Tomean).

Most countries have long official names that have been shortened to forms now preferred by the US Board on Geographic Names. Some examples are Australia (Commonwealth of Australia), Mexico (United Mexican States), and South Africa (Republic of South Africa; this full name would be preferred in some contexts to avoid confusion—for instance, a text on the situation in southern Africa as a whole). Check with a cartographer in OSS/MPG for the proper terminology.

crafts

Do not italicize (or enclose in quotation marks) names of ships, aircraft, or spacecraft.

Examples

seizure of the Pueblo   *a Yankee-class submarine*

launched Soyuz-3   *the Concorde's noise level*

cross-references

The common nouns used in numeral or letter designations of chapters, parts, graphics, tables, and so forth, are not usually parts of titles and are not capitalized in cross-references.

Examples

covered in chapter III, volume I   *(detailed in table A-4)*

refer to appendix B   *disagrees with paragraph 27*

(see figure 13)

dash (or em dash)	The dash is sometimes represented by two hyphens. Note that when the dash falls within a sentence there are no spaces before or after it. Use the dash to mark a sudden break in thought that causes an abrupt change in sentence structure; to set off—for emphasis or clarity—an added explanation or illustration by expanding a phrase occurring in the main clause; and to mark the end of an introductory series. Do not use the dash when other punctuation such as a comma, a colon, or parentheses would suffice. Use the dash to set off parenthetical matter (in this function a pair of dashes can often be replaced by parentheses and should be if there would otherwise be two pairs of dashes within a sentence). If the dash is used to set off material at the end of a sentence, only one dash, at the beginning, is needed. If the material is set off within the sentence, only another dash (not a comma or a semicolon) can be used to end the setoff phrase or clause.

Examples

- *He was a key figure in the successes—as well as the problems, both domestic and international—of Japan's trade policies.*
- *He has three sons—Thomas, 29; Richard, 19; and Henry, 16.*
- *He goes home twice a year—at Christmastime and on his birthday—and he never stays for more than two days.* (In this example, the necessary second dash supersedes the comma that would ordinarily divide the two clauses of this compound sentence.)
- *The report for 1994 (the calendar, not the fiscal, year) led to an angry exchange—unusual for January—in the legislature.*

Use the dash before a final clause that summarizes a series of ideas (in this function the dash is often used interchangeably with the colon).

Example

- *Freedom of speech, freedom of worship, freedom from want, freedom from fear—these are the fundamentals of moral world order.*

Instead of a bullet or as a subseries within a bullet, use a dash to mark the beginning of each part of a block of material (other than quotations) set off by indentation from the rest of the text.

data, media, criteria	These are plural; therefore, use a plural verb.

dates	Write a date without internal punctuation and with day, month, and year in that order.

Examples

- *The base rights will end on 30 April 2008.*

- *Both* (word inserted to avoid starting the sentence with a figure) *10 and 23 November were holidays in 1995.*
- *The March-April spring vacation period empties college campuses.* (Use a hyphen to separate the months.)
- *It snowed on the night of 20-21 February.* (Use a hyphen to separate the days.)
- *The play had a three-week run (25 April–14 May).* (Use an en dash to separate these dates.)

Years

Figures designating a continuous period of two or more years are separated by a hyphen meaning "up to and including." For two years, *and* may be used.

Examples

- *The presidencies of John Adams (1797-1801) and William McKinley (1897-1901) were the only two to span two centuries.*
- *She worked here during the period 1983-94.* (In an expression such as "during the period 1983-94," inclusion of the words "the period" is suggested. The words might then be omitted after the first such use.)

Do not combine *from* or *between* with a hyphen instead of *to* or *and*.

Examples

from 1996 to 2005   *between 1995 and 1999*
from 1995-96 to 2004-05

Do not use a hyphen to date related but separate events occurring in two consecutive years.

Example

- *The first two submarines were launched in 1960 and 1961.*

A hyphen may be used, however, to date events that straddle consecutive years representing a continuous period.

Examples

- *Training of crewmembers took place during the period 1994-95.*
- *She was Minister of Economics (1989-90) before she moved to the Finance Ministry.*

Use a slash (also called diagonal or slant) in a combining form designating a 12-month period occurring in two calendar years, such as a *fiscal year*, an *academic year*, or a *crop year*, and state the type of year and, if necessary, the period covered.

Examples

- *The farm made a profit in the 1993/94 crop year (1 July–30 June) but not in 1994/95.*

- *Registrations for the academic year 1995/96 are still being accepted.*
- *The report covered actual expenditures during fiscal year 1995/96 and made some projections of FY 1997/98 spending.* (Note that the abbreviation FY may be used after the first mention of fiscal year, but do not drop the 19. In this illustration it would be equally clear in the second reference to write simply 1997/98, without the FY or the term it stands for.)

FY

In US Government practice the fiscal year is stated with the calendar year representing the larger portion of the fiscal year. US fiscal year 1995 begins on 1 October 1994 and ends on 30 September 1995. (Japan's fiscal year 1995, on the other hand, begins on 1 April 1995 and ends on 31 March 1996.)

Decades

Decades are usually expressed with the figure for the initial year followed by an *s* but not an apostrophe.

Examples

- *All those submarines were constructed in the 1960s* (not 60s or '60s).
- *1920s vintage; 1920s-vintage car*
- *Our estimates are intended to cover the early and middle 1990s. Your figures deal with the middle and late 1980s.*

Centuries

In certain special contexts, a century may be referred to in a manner similar to that used for decades (*the 1800s, the eighteen hundreds*), but, in most intelligence writing, ordinal numbers (*in the 19th century, 20th-century progress*) would be more appropriate.

Modifiers

Dates as modifiers require careful use.

Examples

- *the 1973 Middle East war* (such wars occurred in other years)
- *the Falklands invasion in 1982* (the 1982 Falklands invasion would imply that the islands were invaded in other years)

---

decimals

Numbers with a decimal point are expressed in figures. Decimal numbers of less than 1 should have a zero before the decimal point except for designations of gun bore or ammunition. Zeros are omitted at the end of a decimal number unless exact measurement is indicated.

Examples

- *0.25 meter* (note that the unit of measure is singular)
- *1.25 centimeters*

- *silver 0.900 fine* (exact measurement*)*
but:
- *.22-caliber cartridge*

---

decimate   Encompasses heavy losses of many kinds. Buildings and tanks are damaged or destroyed, not decimated.

---

defuse, diffuse   *Defuse* means to remove a fuse (or *fuze*) from a weapon or, nonliterally, to deintensify, as in *to defuse a crisis. Diffuse* means to spread around, to scatter.

---

degrees   Always express *degrees* in numerals.

Example
- *longitude 77 degrees 4 minutes 6 seconds east* (note: no commas*)*

---

depart   Requires a preposition.

Example
- *She will depart from Dulles today.*

---

derivatives   Once formed, a compound can form derivatives that usually retain the hyphenated or solid form of the original.

Examples

coldbloodedness	*ill-advisedly*	*stick-to-it-iveness*
cost-effectiveness	*praiseworthiness*	*X-rayed*
footnoting	*railroader*	

---

designators   There are, in general terms, two principal types of designators: the indigenous name or number used by the manufacturer or the country of origin and the nickname (arbitrary, nonindigenous name) assigned by NATO.

Indigenous

Indigenous names are given by manufacturing firms or producing countries to their products. These may be coined word names, alphanumeric designators, or model numbers. The spelling of an indigenous name follows the style used by the country of origin; if the name is a word, only the initial letter is capitalized.

Examples

the French Mystere aircraft	*the US Tomahawk*
the B-52 bomber	*the Boeing 747*

Letters within indigenous Russian aircraft designators correspond to names of design bureaus or designers. Designators, therefore, are rendered in capital and lowercase letters.

Examples

Yak	*Tu*	*Mi*
An	*Su*	*Il*
but:		
MiG		

Nicknames

Arbitrary nonindigenous nicknames are assigned by NATO or the US Intelligence Community. These are usually rendered as regular proper nouns. Capitalize only the first letter of NATO designators. (Note: FROG and HAWK are acronyms, not nicknames.)

Examples

Foxbat	*Kangaroo*	*Scaleboard*
Backfire	*Dog House*	*Scud*

Variants and modifications are designated by alphabetical or numerical elements following the name.

Examples

Flogger B	*FROG-7*
Backfire C	*SS-12/-22 Mod 2*

Names for classes of ships also are written with initial capitals only.

Examples

Victor-II-class SSN	*Kresta-class CG*	*Riga-class FF*
Kiev-class CV	*Yankee-class SSBN*	*Balzam-class AGI*

Use hyphens in the compounds designating Russian submarine classes when the compounds are used adjectivally. If the meaning is clear, refer to these submarines by the class designator alone. (In CIA publications the full designator, not its first letter, is preferred: *Delta-class* (not D-class), *Yankee-class* (not Y-class). Note, however, that the designator is spelled with only the first letter capitalized, not in all capital letters. Designators for Russian submarines are as follows: *Akula, Alfa, Bravo, Charlie, Delta, Echo, Foxtrot, Golf, Hotel, India, Juliett, Kilo, Lima, Mike, November, Oscar, Papa, Romeo, Sierra, Tango, Typhoon* (not a phonetic), *Uniform, Victor, Whiskey, Yankee,* and *Zulu.*

The same rules apply essentially to surface ship classes (*Komar*, *Osa*) and non-Russian submarine classes (*Han*, *Xia*).

Examples

- *Yankee-class, Delta-class, Victor-class*
- *Echo-II-class, Charlie-I-class* (two hyphens*)*
- *submarines of the Yankee class (*no hyphen*)*
- *a Delta-class unit, a Delta-II-class unit*
- *Delta and Yankee units (*acceptable to omit the word class*)*
- *a Victor tracking a Yankee*
- *Four Yankees, two Delta-IIs, and a Victor have been observed in the submarine yard.*
- *The characteristics of the Delta-I and -II were compared.*

Special care must be taken when a class name is derived from the known indigenous name of a specific vessel, often the first in its class. The distinction between *the frigate Lulubelle* and *a Lulubelle-class frigate* should be immediately clear.

Note that neither italic type nor quotation marks is used with the name of a specific vessel.

Interim Designators

Interim designators are used for newly detected models of equipment or variants of previously identified models. The intention is to use these only until a uniform US designator is assigned; the indigenous model number is learned; or it is established that the object is a one-of-a-kind, experimental model. A statement of explanation is, therefore, helpful to the reader.

Abbreviations for Equipment

Most equipment abbreviations and isolated letters in model identifiers are rendered in solid capital letters.

Examples

transporter-erector-launcher (TEL)	*M-1974 armored personnel carrier (APC)*
AK47 Russian rifle	*M16 US machinegun*

Unpronounceable mixes of letters and numbers are rendered with solid capitals.

Examples

ATS-59 tractor	*MDK-2 ditcher*

The gun-bore size (caliber in personal weapons) is expressed in millimeters, with a hyphen, and is always lowercased.

Example

• *-mm*

Type

If this word occurs as part of the known indigenous designator, the initial letter is capitalized. The *t* is lowercased if the type designator is used for reporting purposes only and is neither indigenous nor approved by NATO.

Examples

76-mm Type 54 field gun   *type IV warhead van*

If the writer is describing a new and unnamed item by associating it with a similar known model, the word *type* is lowercased.

Example

• *the PMP-type pontoon bridge*

Because this construction is informal, it should be avoided whenever possible. When appropriate, it is preferable to add an accurate qualifier preceding the designator.

Examples

what probably are T-62 tanks   *possibly a modified T-62 tank*

Plurals of Designators

If the full name of an object is used, the plural is formed on the noun. When the noun is omitted or the abbreviation is used, the plural is formed on the element acting as a noun.

Examples

six Hind helicopters (six Hinds)   *15 M-1974 APCs (15 M-1974s)*

The apostrophe is inserted before a lowercase *s* to form the plurals of single letters and digits. It is not inserted before the *s* in the plurals of groups of letters or hyphenated letter-number combinations unless needed to enhance comprehension—for example, if the combination ends with a lowercase letter.

Examples

Flogger B's   *SS-N-4s (but SS-N-3a's)*
Mod 2's (but all Mods of the SS-11)   *Pershing Ia's (but Pershing IIs)*
H-Is and H-IIs

Because the words in NATO designators are used as names and not in a literal sense, the plural is always formed by the addition of the lowercased *s*.

Examples

| 17 Bisons | four Coots | 23 Crustys |

Use of the generic noun will produce a smoother, less jarring sentence.

Examples

| 17 Bison bombers | four Coot transports | 23 Crusty aircraft |

---

diacritical marks

Are used only on maps, in *The World Factbook*, and, occasionally, in papers, although their use does not conform to DI text style.

---

die

Do not write if he dies, insert *in office* or *before the end of his term*, or even say simply *when he dies*.

**different from,
differs from**

Different from is correct; different than is not. Better yet, *differs from*.

---

dilemma

Involves a choice between two equally unsatisfactory courses of action. It is not the proper word to use when you mean simply a predicament or a troublesome decision.

---

dimensions

Express size in length, width, and height. The length is the greater of the two horizontal dimensions. Any dimension expressing diameter or depth should be so specified.

Examples
- *a garage measuring 30 by 18 by 12 meters (or 30 by 18 meters by 12 meters high)*
- *a 6- by 3-meter trailer*
- *a canister 15 meters long and 1.2 meters in diameter*

Note that a vertical measurement is always *height* or *high*.

**diplomatic and
consular units**

Capitalize the full or shortened name of a specific embassy, mission, or consulate, but not those words when used generally.

Examples
- *the British Embassy, the Embassy*
- *the British Embassies in Paris and Rome*
- *the US Mission, a spokesman for the Mission*
- *the French Consulate, the Consulate, during Consulate hours*

- *Foreign Service*
- *Interests Section*
but:
- *reports from African embassies*
- *employees skilled in consulate operations*
- *members of diplomatic missions*
- *US embassy guards in the Communist states*

---

disburse, disperse

Disburse refers to the release of funds.

Example

- *The bursar disbursed the funds on Friday.*

Disperse means to scatter.

Example

- *The Bhutan Air Force dispersed all its aircraft on Friday.*

---

documents

Spell out references to laws, statutes, legislative bills, documents, resolutions, reports, articles, sections, and so forth. When used in conjunction with a figure, the word *number* may be abbreviated, using a period.

Examples

- *House Bill 416*
- *Article 1*
- *Senate Report 214 Paragraph 8 Section 13* (note no commas)
- *Resolution No. 25*

---

domestic, indigenous

Domestic and *indigenous* are synonymous in some senses but not all. Modifying *production*, for example, they both define it as homegrown, or related to the country concerned. Modifying *animal*, however, the words diverge in meaning, *domestic* meaning domesticated or tamed, *indigenous* connoting native to or naturally occurring in the country or region concerned.

each	As a subject, *each* takes a singular verb and singular related pronouns. If, however, *each* follows a plural subject, the verb is plural.
East Asia	Preferred over Far East except in the Russian Far East.
East-West	Usually refers in international politics to relations between the Communist and non-Communist worlds. But West and East can also connote distinction between places and especially peoples with cultures of, respectively, European and non-European (usually Asian) origin.
economic growth	The rate of economic growth may remain the same, increase, or slow. When the growth is negative, the gross national product (GNP)—not economic growth—is declining.
election	Singular in most cases.

Examples

national election	*general election*	*presidential election*

but:
- *presidential and legislative elections*
- *municipal elections in several parts of the country*

ellipsis	An ellipsis (the omission of words within quoted material) is represented by three periods with spaces between the words and each other. When in the middle of a quotation an ellipsis occurs at the end of a sentence, a fourth period (or other punctuation, if appropriate) precedes the spaced periods. When only part of a sentence is quoted, periods to show omission are not required at the beginning or the end.

Examples

- *The President began his address with the observation that in 1776 "our fathers brought forth . . . a new nation, conceived in liberty and dedicated to the proposition" of equality for everyone.*
- *In his words, "we cannot consecrate . . . this ground. The brave men . . . who struggled here . . . have consecrated it. . . . The world . . . can never forget what they did here."*

emigrate, immigrate, migrate	*Emigrate* is to leave a place permanently and is usually followed by *from*. *Immigrate* is to come to a place permanently and is usually followed by *to*. *Migrate* embraces both. When a sentence includes both the place of departure and the place of arrival, *immigrate* is usually omitted.

Example

* *He emigrated from Sweden to Italy.*

en dash	**In Proper Noun Compounds**

In a unit modifier made up of proper adjectives or proper nouns of which one or more is a compound, the en dash (or space hyphen space) is used between the parts.

Examples

* *North American–South American sphere*
* *Winston-Salem–Pointe Claire telephone call* (or *call between Winston-Salem and Pointe Claire*)
* *Saudi Arabia–United Arab Emirates border* (or *border between Saudi Arabia and the United Arab Emirates*)
* *Health Department–sponsored program* (or *program sponsored by the Health Department*)
* *post–World War II policies* (or *policies after World War II*)
* *pro–INF Treaty groups* (or *groups favoring the INF Treaty*)
* *SS-19–type silos* (or *silos of the SS-19 type*)

but:

* *Echo-II-class submarine* (use two hyphens, not a hyphen and an en dash, because this is a special category)

and:

* *defense-industry-based engineers*

also:

* *a vice-president-elect,* but *the Vice President–elect; a prime-minister-designate,* but *the Prime Minister–designate*

Use an en dash instead of a hyphen in a timespan joining compound elements.

Example

* *July 1995–June 1996*

endings	**O Endings**

Nouns ending in *o* preceded by a vowel add *s* to form the plural; nouns ending in *o* preceded by a consonant add *es* to form the plural, except as indicated in the following selected list. (Note that this rule excludes such frequently used words as *cargoes, embargoes, fiascoes,* and *torpedoes.* Note also that *Tornados* is the plural of the aircraft name, but *tornadoes* is the plural of the common noun.)

Examples

commandos	magnetos	solos
dynamos	mementos	tobaccos
egos	mestizos	twos
escudos	octavos	virtuosos
ghettos	provisos	zeros
kimonos	salvos	

Endings -yze, -ize, and -ise

A verb whose last three letters are pronounced like "eyes" is usually spelled in one of three ways. The letter *l* is usually followed by *yze* when the related noun ends in *lysis*.

Examples

analyze (analysis)   paralyze (paralysis)

Most other words in this class end in *ize*.

Exceptions

advertise	devise	incise
advise	disguise	revise
arise	enfranchise	rise
chastise	exercise	supervise
comprise	exorcise	surmise
compromise	franchise	surprise
despise	improvise	televise

Endings -sede, -ceed, and -cede

A verb with a final syllable that sounds like "seed" is usually spelled in one of three ways. As shown below, only one such word ends in *sede*, only three end in *ceed*, and the others end in *cede*.

Examples

supersede	exceed	accede
	proceed	concede
	succeed	intercede
		precede

Adverbs Ending in -ly

Do not use a hyphen in a two-word unit modifier in which the first word is an adverb ending in ly.

Examples

- *recently designed logo*
- *wholly owned subsidiary*

but:

- *only-child complex*
- *lonely-hearts club*

---

ensure, assure, insure

Use *ensure* to mean make certain. *Assure* applies to persons. Save *insure* for what insurance companies do.

---

equally, as

These two words should not be used together in the same sentence when you are making comparisons. Drop *equally* when you are comparing two persons or groups or two things.

Example

- *He is as ineffective as his predecessor.*

Drop *as* when you name only one person or group or one thing in the sentence.

Example

- *They are equally ineffective.*

---

equivalent, equal

Equivalent applies to two or more things that have a qualitative similarity. *Equal* emphasizes precise quantitative likeness.

---

escalate, accelerate, intensify

Escalate means to increase by successive stages. Do not use *escalate* when you mean simply *accelerate* or *intensify*.

---

ethnic cleansing, atrocity

Try using words like *atrocity*. If you have to use the term *ethnic cleansing* (for example, when one Balkan charges another with it) place the phrase within quotation marks.

---

even

If *even* (as an adverb) ends up in the wrong place it can distort meaning, and its proper placement in a sentence requires care.

Examples

- *Even the Secretary was not disturbed by the threats* (and, if anybody would be, it would be he).
- *The Secretary was not even disturbed by the threats* (in fact, he was more or less unaffected).
- *The Secretary was not disturbed even by the threats* (much less by other things).

evidence	Should be defined as specifically as possible in your reporting. What is the source of the information? When was it obtained? How reliable do you believe it is? Avoid phrases like available evidence indicates.
exclamation point	In CIA formal issuances, do not use the exclamation point.
exile	Except for diplomatic exile, a person is *exiled from* a country, not to a country.
extra words	Should be avoided.

Examples

in the event that (if)	*it is possible that (may)*
the manner in which (how)	*it is highly likely that (probably)*
due to the fact that (because)	*at that point in time (then)*
in regard to (about)	*at the present time (now)*
in the near future (soon)	*currently in progress (going on)*
subsequent to (after)	*never before in the past (never)*
are in a position to (can)	*the majority of (most)*
whether or not (whether)	

fake analysis	Phrases like the following detract from any serious presentation.

Examples

anything can happen	*it is too early to tell*
it is not possible to predict	*it remains to be seen*
further developments are to be expected	*only the future will tell*

feel, evaluate, feel different	As a verb, *feel* can mean to be aware of something instinctively or emotionally. Intelligence analysts, however, should *evaluate*, not feel. As a linking verb, *feel* is followed by an adjective when describing a personal condition—*I feel bad.* You *feel different* when your condition has changed from bad to good.

fewer, less	The word *fewer* should be used only when an actual count can be made. The word *less* should be used when referring to quantity.

Examples

- We have *fewer* staff members than we had last year.
- They made *fewer* mistakes with the new calculating machine.
- We have *less* trouble now than we had before.

fill-ins (transition phrases)	In careful composition, words and phrases such as the following should be reserved for those few occasions when they are needed.

Examples

also	*in connection with*	*on the other hand*
as noted	*indeed*	*essentially*
at the same time	*in this context*	*significantly*
basically	*of course*	*with reference to*

first, second, third	And other designators of numerical order are preferred to firstly, secondly, and thirdly.

fiscal, monetary	*Fiscal* applies to a budget, *monetary* to currency.

flammable, inflammable	*Flammable* is the preferred word when you are describing a combustible substance. However, a situation or a temperament is *inflammable*.

footnote references	An asterisk or a superior footnote reference number or letter normally follows all punctuation marks except a dash but falls inside a closing parenthesis or bracket if it applies only to the matter within the parentheses or brackets. A comma is omitted between superior figures or letters in footnote references.

forceful, forcible	*Forceful* means vigorous, strong, effective. *Forcible* suggests the exertion of force, often the use of physical violence.
forego, forgo	*Forego* is to precede in time or place. If you are doing without something, *forgo* the *e*.
foreign words	The need for italicizing or translating depends on whether the non-English word or phrase has been adapted into English, has not been anglicized but is reasonably familiar to American readers, is the title of a publication or work of art, is the name of an organization, or is otherwise governed by some special consideration.

Anglicized Words

Do not italicize (or use diacritical marks in) foreign words and phrases that have been naturalized into English. For a specific anglicized foreign word, check the Compound Words/Spelling section.

Familiar Foreign Words

Italicize but do not translate foreign words and expressions that have not been anglicized but are familiar to American readers or are easily understood by virtue of their similarity to English (an English equivalent is preferred unless the foreign expression has a special meaning).

Example

• *The speaker was shouted down by crowds chanting, "Democracia, democracia!"*

Other Foreign Words

When an unfamiliar non-English word is used in ordinary text, italicize it and follow it with a translation in parentheses. This need not be a literal translation if a freer interpretation or explanation would be more helpful to the reader. The translation is not italicized unless it constitutes a title of a publication or work of art.

Examples

• *The achievement of* enosis *(union) with Greece is the all-consuming goal of one segment of the Cypriot population.*
• *Manzoni's* I promessi sposi *(The Betrothed) is required reading for Dr. Caino's course in Italian literature.*

Foreign Terms

The name of a foreign institution is spelled out in English if possible, but the commonly used abbreviation may be used even if it is drawn from the foreign wording.

Example

• *Polish United Workers' Party (PZPR)*

Foreign Phrases

Do not hyphenate a foreign phrase used as a unit modifier.

Example

• *bona fide testimony*

---

foreword

Is the name for something written, usually by someone other than the author, to appear at the beginning of an article or book.

---

fractions

Fractions are written out, with a hyphen in both noun and adjective forms.

Examples

• *three-fourths* (or *three-quarters*) *of a kilometer*—Fractional quantities such as this one may sound plural, but they take a singular verb. The same is true of any quantitative expression in which the emphasis is on its meaning as a single unit of measure: for example, money ($500 is too expensive), time (two years is too long), and distance (between 70 and 110 km is all right).
• *a two-thirds majority; a majority of two-thirds*
• *one-fifth of the electorate; one-tenth; one-twentieth* (or *a fifth, a tenth, a twentieth*)
• *second-quarter earnings*
• *first-half-1995 election*
but:
• *a quarter century*
• *a quarter of a lifetime*
• *the second quarter of 1996, the first three quarters of 1996, earnings for second quarter 1996*
• *first half 1996* (*of* is implied, no hyphen)

Free World

Use only in quoted matter.

gender

Although efforts are ongoing, new words and phrases have been introduced into the English language to counter the predominance of masculine forms.

Examples

business persons	*firefighter*	*layperson*
chairperson, chair	*mail carrier*	*member of Congress*
flight attendant	*anchor, newscaster*	*Diet members*
police officer		

No completely satisfactory substitute has been found for the pronouns *he*, *his*, and *him*. Repeating *he or she* or *his or hers* or *him or her* can become tiresome. The best solution is to use the plural.

Example

• *All representatives must cast their ballots.*

If this is impractical, stick with *one* or *he or she.* Avoid s/he.

genus, species

Capitalize a specific genus name, but lowercase the species name.

Example

• *Homo sapiens*

geographic names

Our authority for the spelling of place names is the Cartography Center in OSS/MPG. MPG interprets for CIA the rulings of the US Board on Geographic Names. Be sure that the spellings of place names in the text of the paper agree with those on the map(s). If the approved spelling is markedly different from a more familiar and recognizable spelling, in the first reference insert the familiar name in parentheses after the BGN name. In subsequent references you can use only the familiar name.

Examples

Khalij Qabis (Gulf of Gabes)   *Al Biqa' (Bekaa Valley)*

Follow *The World Factbook* and the MPG cartographer's advice in the use of hyphens and apostrophes in transliterations.

Examples

Cote d'Ivoire   *N'Djamena*   *Komsomol'sk*

Diacritical marks used to spell place names on a map, however, are usually omitted in the text.

geographic terms	**Direction**

A geographic term used to denote mere direction or position on the earth is not a proper name and is not capitalized.

Examples

- *north, south, east, west, south-central, far north*
- *55°45´ north latitude, 37°35´ east longitude*
- *northerly, eastward, far western*
- *east coast, southern France, central Europe*
- *hemisphere, the polar region, polar icecap; the Arctic Circle, the Arctic region* (but lowercase as descriptive adjective: *arctic conditions, clothing,* and so forth)

Capitalize *Earth, Moon*, and *Sun* only in extraterrestrial contexts.

Examples

Earth orbit	*Moon landing*	*orbit the Sun*
but:		
the earth's topography	*moonlight*	*sunshine*

Proper Name

Geographic terms often become part of a proper name for a definite region, geographic feature, or political grouping and are capitalized.

Examples

- *the West, the East, Western countries, East-West dialogue*
- *the Western Hemisphere, the North Pole, San Andreas Fault, the Equator*
- *North Atlantic*
- *the Continent (*continental Europe only*)* but *the contiguous United States (*meaning the first 48 states*)* and *the continental United States (*meaning the first 48 states plus Alaska*)*
- *Greater New York, Metropolitan New York (*but *New York metropolitan area)*

North and South, capitalized, are often used as abbreviations of the two Koreas or to refer, respectively, to the developed and developing nations, as in "the North-South dialogue."

Intelligence Reporting Divisions

Some capitalized geographic terms are used to divide the world into groups of countries for purposes of intelligence reporting.

Examples

- *Middle East* or *Middle Eastern* (preferred over Near East, Mideast)

- *Baltic states*
- *North Africa (*occasionally *North-Central Africa)*
- *Sub-Saharan Africa, sub-Saharan state, Pan-Saharan state*
- *North Rhine–Westphalia*
- *North-West Frontier Province*
- *South China*
- *West Africa, East Africa,* but *southern Africa (*South Africa refers only to the republic*)*
- *South Asia (*sometimes *Southwest* or *Southeast Asia)*
- *East Asia (*preferred over Far East, but *the Russian Far East)*
- *Oceania (*note also *North, South Pacific, the Pacific Rim* but *eastern, western Pacific)*
- *Western Europe, West European, Eastern Europe, East European*
- *Latin America, Middle America, Central America*

Some countries fall into more than one category, depending on the context. In some reports, countries logically belonging in a geographic category are grouped separately by some other criterion, such as membership in NATO. Often the Communist countries are arbitrarily separated from the East Asia category for purposes of reporting economic statistics. The Arab states are frequently treated as a group in papers on the Middle East. And the terms Middle America and Central America are not synonymous. Be careful, therefore, to explain any such groupings or any deviations from normal geographic categories in a prefatory note or footnote.

Geological Terms

A structural term is not capitalized, even if preceded by a name.

Examples

arch (Cincinnati arch)   *basin (Caribbean basin)*   *continental shelf*

---

glossaries

If glossaries are of abbreviations and acronyms, both the short form and the definition should be rendered as they would be in midsentence.

Green

Capitalize when referring to political and other groups opposed to environmental pollution, even in the general sense.

Example

- *a coalition of Green parties, the Greens*

hackneyed phrases	Phrases like the following have been so overused that they are becoming meaningless cliches.

Examples

keep their options open	*nonstarters*
assume the mantle of office	*heightened tensions*
refurbish his tarnished image	*dire straits*
triggered new developments	*far-reaching implications*
generates further disagreement	*considered judgment*
hammer out a compromise	*widely held perception*
hit the campaign trail	*a likely scenario*
viable alternatives	*geared up for action*
net effect of the decision	*potential chokepoint*
broad outlines of the case	*bottom line*

hanged, hung	*Hanged* is the past tense of hang when referring to an execution; *hung* is the proper past tense in all other meanings.
hardly	Has the force of a negative; be careful to avoid an inadvertent double negative.
headers	In formal writing for finished intelligence, a seven-level hierarchy may be used:

- *Main title.*
- *Super A head.*
- *A head.*
- *B head.*
- *C head.*
- *D head.*
- *Text*

The title, super A head, and A head are the only levels that need their own classification.

historic, historical	*Historic* means famous in history.

Example

- *Gettysburg was the scene of a historic battle.*

Historical refers to general events of the past.

Example

- *She presented a historical review of the Middle East.*

hopefully	Means with hope. Avoid using hopefully in the sense of *it is to be hoped, in the hope of,* or *let us hope*. *Regretfully, mercifully, interestingly*, and other subjective words are vulnerable to the same kind of abuse.

hyphen

Improvised Compounds

Hyphenate improvised compounds.

Examples

need-to-know	*technical know-how*
first-come-first-served basis	*hard-and-fast rule*
classroom full of know-it-alls	*bread-and-butter issue*

Verb Forms

Hyphenate the verb forms of noun forms written as two words.

Examples

- *turn a cold shoulder (to cold-shoulder an idea)*
- *proof with blue pencils (to blue-pencil galleys)*
- *missile in flight test (to flight-test a missile)*

impact	Use *impact* as an intransitive verb. A missile impacts *on* or *in* a target area.
important	Use *more important* rather than more importantly.
in	As an adverb in titles, capitalize *in*.
incident	Applies to a minor occurrence or an event of only momentary importance, not a major conflict.

Example

- *A border incident took place yesterday when a small patrol entered the neutral zone.*

incredible, incredulous	*Incredible* means not believable; *incredulous* means skeptical.

Examples

- *His explanation was incredible.*
- *She gave him an incredulous stare.*

indefinite articles	The indefinite article *a* is used before a consonant and an aspirated *h*; the article *an* is used before silent *h* and all vowels except *u* pronounced as in *usual* and *o* pronounced as in *one*.

Examples

a historical review	*a union*	*an onion*
a hotel	*an herb* (but *a herbicide*)	*an oyster*
a humble man	*an honor*	
a once-over	*an hour*	

When a group of initials pronounced as letters begins with *b, c, d, g, j, k, p, q, t, u, v, w, y,* or *z*, each having a consonant sound, the article *a* is used.

Examples

a BGN compilation	*a TQM decision*
a CIA position	*a UPI dispatch*

When a group of initials pronounced as letters begins with *f, h, i a, e,, l, m, n, o, r, s,* or *x,* each having a vowel sound, the indefinite article *an* is used.

Examples

an FBIS transliteration   *an NBC program*

an HHS report   *an RSFSR ministry*

an MRV system   *an SLBM system*

When initials form an acronym that is pronounced as a word, the use of *a* or *an* is determined by the sound.

Examples

a HAWK missile   *an NPIC contribution*

a MIRV system   *an NREM sleep*

a NASA launch   *an UNCTAD report*

If pronunciation of an abbreviation is variable or borders on slang, choose the article appropriate to sounding the group of initials as letters.

Examples

• *an AAA battalion,* not a AAA (as though pronounced "triple A") battalion
• *an SLBM system,* not a SLBM (as though pronounced "slubbum") system
but:
• *a SLCM* (as though pronounced "slikkum") *system*

---

indicate   A derivative of indication, suggests a conclusion based on specific information.

---

individual   Not always a desirable synonym for person. *Individual* serves best as distinguished from *group*.

Example

• *The police are searching for the group or individual responsible.*

---

infinitives   Split when you must, but make sure that clarity or the flow of the sentence demands the split. If you use an infinitive in a title, be sure to capitalize the *To*.

---

injuries, casualties   Are suffered or sustained, not received or taken.

---

in order to   Often begins an adverbial phrase in the middle of a sentence, but at the beginning you can usually do without the first two words.

insure, ensure, assure	Save *insure* for what insurance companies do. *Ensure* means to make certain. *Assure* applies to persons.
in terms of	Can be replaced by *at, in, for*, or *by*.
italics	Italic type (or underscoring) must be chosen sparingly to avoid the excessive use that defeats the primary purpose of italicizing: to give prominence or emphasis to particular words and phrases. Use italic type for titles of books, periodicals, or works of art (including the performing arts—plays, compositions, broadcasts, films, and so forth). Selective use of italic type is also effective in publications design (such as the examples in this style guide).
	Do not italicize names of crafts.

lack   Is not followed by for.

Example
- *The French do not lack* (omit for) *a sense of their grandeur.*

Latin abbreviations   The utility of certain Latin abbreviations (such as *op. cit., et al.,* and *ibid.*) should be avoided except in footnotes and bibliographies. Particularly troublesome are *e.g.* and *i.e.* Instead, lean toward *for example* or *for instance* (instead of e.g.) and *that is* (instead of i.e.)—all three phrases followed by a comma. The same problem arises with *viz.*—try *namely* or *that is* (followed by a comma). Another Latin abbreviation to be watched is *etc.*, because it is, in general, appropriate to informal writing but not appropriate to formal writing. If these abbreviations are used, they retain the periods and are not italicized. Nor is *versus* italicized, either spelled out (preferred in a title or heading) or abbreviated (*vs.*).

latter, former   *Latter* and *former* refer to one of only two persons or things or collections of either.

letter or number elements   Do not use a hyphen in a unit modifier containing a letter or numeral as its second element.

Examples

annex B maps	*Mod 3 missile*
Article III provisions	*number 2 fuel oil*
grade A milk	*Proposition 13 backlash*
level 4 alert	*Type 59 tank*

This rule, however, does not apply to certain terms established by long usage for military aircraft and naval ships.

Examples

An-22	*SA-8*
Kresta-I	*Su-7*
MiG-19	*Yak-40*
Osa-II	

but:

Mirage 2000-7	*Scud B*	*Scud C*

like, as	*Like* and *as* can properly be used in making comparisons, but *like*, a preposition, governs nouns, pronouns, and incomplete clauses, while *as*, a conjunction, governs full clauses.

Examples
- *He behaves like a child.*
- *He behaves as a child would behave.*

likely	As an adverb, *likely* must be preceded by a qualifier.

Example
- *She will most likely win the election.*

As an adjective, *likely* must be followed by an infinitive.

Example
- *He is likely to blow the operation.*

likewise	Is an adverb and cannot properly be used as a substitute for and.

majority	A *majority* means more than 50 percent. *Majority* takes a singular verb when the sense is oneness.

Example

- *The majority of the Senate supports the measure.*

When the individuality of the members is stressed, the verb is plural.

Example

- *The majority of the Senators are from rural districts.*

margin	*Margin*, not majority, is what you call the number of legislative seats by which the majority exceeds the minority.

Example

- *The Prime Minister's party, with 220 seats, has a 20-seat margin over the opposition's 200 seats.*

military	As a noun *military* can be singular or plural—be consistent within a paper. If in doubt, consider it plural.

military forces	Capitalize the full proper name (or reasonable translations and approximations of the proper name) of a military force or service as well as the shortened form of that name.

Examples

- *the Egyptian Army, the Army, an Army engineer;* but *Egyptian artillery units; army, division,* or *regiment level*
- *the People's Liberation Army, the Army, the PLA;* but *Chinese ground forces*
- *the Royal Air Force, the Air Force, the RAF, an Air Force pilot*
- *the Strategic Rocket Forces, the SRF* (not the Forces)
- *the Russian Navy, the Navy, a Navy officer;* but *Russian naval forces, a naval officer*
- *Israel Defense Forces (IDF)* but *army, air force,* or *navy* in reference to that of Israel

This rule does not apply to individual units in the matter of capitalizing the shortened form of the name.

Examples

- *the 3rd Army, the army* (in Russian context the terms *army* and *front* mean echelons—either is uppercased only when referring to a specific unit or command)
- *the 7th Fleet, the fleet*
- *the 28th Division, the division*
- *the 1028th Brigade, the brigade*

Nor does it apply to a reference, other than a proper name, to military services as a group, to a general reference to one kind of service in the plural form, or to any general reference.

Examples

- *the Russian armed forces*
- *the British military establishment*
- *the infantry, the artillery, the submarine forces*
- *US naval forces*
- *the navies of the Mediterranean NATO members*
- *a navy (an army, an air force) to be proud of*
- *Russian-supplied air force (naval, ground force) equipment*

but:

- *the German and Slovak Air Forces, the Greek and Turkish Navies* (specific services referred to by proper names in plural form—refer to *The World Factbook*)

---

millions and billions

Numbers over 999,999 are rounded unless an exact amount must be stated. Spell out *million* or *billion* preceded by a figure rounded usually to no more than two decimal places. This form of rounding is never applied to *thousands*.

Examples

- *The US population is about 240 million.*
- *World population now exceeds 4.7 billion.*
- *American casualties in World War II totaled 1,078,162.*
- *More than 16.35 million Americans served in World War II—more than three times the 4.74 million in World War I.*
- *The Veterans Administration planned to spend about $18.4 billion in 1994.*
- *Estimates range between $10 million and $20 million* (not *between $10 and $20 million*).

but:

- *The cost is estimated at $10-20 million.*

Mod

Acceptable in formal writing about weapons to designate different versions (models) of a weapon system.

Examples

the SS-11 Mod 2   all Mods of the SS-11

---

momentarily

Applies to a fleeting instant; it does not mean at any moment.

money

US Dollars

Values expressed in US money are given in figures preceded by a dollar sign. Ordinarily, there is no need for the initials US to precede the dollar sign unless the context could allow the reader to assume that dollars other than US dollars were meant. If this is the case and the dollar amounts appear throughout the text, consider adding a footnote such as "Money values in this paper are in US dollars unless otherwise indicated." The word *dollars* is used in an indefinite expression with no figure given or if some definition of the word is needed such as the year to which the dollar value applies. The word *cents* is used for amounts less than a dollar.

Examples

- *Russia spent nearly $50 million to develop the system.*
- *The average wage earner in Sweden pays $5,280 annually in income tax, or about 62 cents for every dollar earned.*
- *The Australian motorist pays about US $6.00 for 15 liters (about 4 US gallons) of gasoline.*
- *Each unit now costs several hundred dollars.*
- *We estimate the system cost the equivalent of 50-60 billion 1987 dollars.*
- *The cost for printing each page was 89 cents.*

Foreign Money

When values are expressed in foreign money, use figures except for indefinite amounts.

Examples

- *The Israeli-British talks set the unit price at 1,250 pounds sterling (3,065 Israeli pounds).*
- *The construction costs averaged 5 rubles per capita.*
- *The fare is only 1 deutsche mark.*

but:

- *Souvenirs in London will cost a few pounds more (sterling is understood).*

more than, fewer than, over/under

Over and *under* describe location; use *more than* and *fewer than* with numbers. For time, use *during*, *from*, or *while*.

Examples

- *The system has improved during the past year.*
- *Inflation is up 10 percent from a year ago.*

Muslims/Muhammad

Muslims, not Moslems, are adherents of Islam. They are followers of the prophet Muhammad, not Mohammed.

nationalities, tribes, and other groups	Capitalize the names of racial, linguistic, tribal, and religious groupings such as the following. Check *The World Factbook* for specific groupings in a country.

Examples

African-American	*Indian*	*Mormon*
Arab	*Indo-Chinese*	*Native American*
Asian	*Indo-European*	*Nordic*
Asian-American	*Jewish*	*Oriental*
Berber	*KwaZulu*	*Polynesian*
Bushman	*Magyar*	*Pygmy*
Caucasian	*Malay*	*Zulu*
Colored (South Africa only)	*Maori*	
Creole	*Mongol*	

neither . . . nor	When the elements in a *neither . . . nor* construction are singular, the verb is singular; when they are plural, the verb is plural. When the elements differ in number, the verb is determined by the number of the nearer (or nearest) element.

Example

• *Neither he nor his advisers understand these matters.*

Be sure that the words affected by *neither . . . nor* are in proper balance.

Examples

• *She specified neither time nor place.*
• *She neither specified the time nor designated the place.*

nonaligned countries	Belong to alliances of neither West nor East, and they are advocates or opponents of selective policies of both sides.

nonconventional, unconventional	*Nonconventional* refers to high-tech weaponry short of nuclear explosives.

Example

• *Fuel-air bombs constitute an effective form of nonconventional weapons.*

Unconventional means not bound by convention.

Example

• *Isadora Duncan was an unconventional woman.*

none	*None* is singular when used in the sense of no one or not one.

Example

- *None of those delegates was elected party chair.*

If *none* applies to more than one person or thing, use a plural verb.

Example

- *None of those delegates were expected to be nominated.*

The object of the prepositional *of* phrase following *none* is usually the best indicator of whether *none* is singular or plural.

Examples

- *None of the cake was eaten.*
- *None of the cookies were eaten.*

North-South	Refers in international politics to relations between industrialized and developing nations.

number of	A phrase that is too imprecise in some contexts.

Example

- *A number of troops were killed.* (If you do not know how many, say *an unknown number*.)

Number of, when preceded by *the*, usually takes a singular verb.

Example

- *The number of mistakes is small.*

When preceded by *a*, *number of* generally takes a plural verb and means several.

Example

- *A number of the mistakes are due to carelessness.*

numbers	**Numbers Under 10**

Spell out most numbers of less than 10. However, use figures for numbers under 10 if they are decimal numbers, ages of persons, percentages, specific amounts of money, or numbers used with units of measure other than time.

Examples

- *For five years the county has provided free preschool classes for 5-year-olds.*
- *He walked 6 kilometers every 2.5 days (*but *every two days).*
- *She spent 8 percent of her time in Europe.*
- *He overspent his daily allowance by an average of $7.00*

Numbers of 10 or More

Except in the first word of a sentence, write numbers of 10 or more in figures.

Examples

- *Her tour covered 11 countries in 16 days.*
- *Sixteen days of traveling left him exhausted. (*Or reword: *He was exhausted after 16 days of traveling.)*

Mixes of Numbers Above and Below 10

Combinations of numbers on either side of 10 follow the basic rules governing numbers set forth above.

Examples

- *The estimate covers the period five to 10 years from now.*
- *The measure lacked three of the 34 votes needed for approval.*
- *The attack involved about 200 troops, 12 tanks, and two aircraft.*

Ordinal Numbers

The rules governing cardinal numbers generally apply to ordinal numbers, except that military units are always designated by figures (again, unless the figure unavoidably comes at the beginning of a sentence), and fractions are usually written out.

Examples

First Congress, 82nd Congress
ninth century, 20th century
seventh region, 17th region
fifth anniversary, 50th anniversary
first grade, 11th grade
3rd Army
2nd Infantry Division
but:
XII Corps (Army usage)

323rd Fighter Wing
1028th Brigade
9th Naval District
7th Fleet
32nd Battalion
13th Party Congress

Indefinite Numbers

Except with words such as *about, nearly, more than*, and *approximately*, references to quantities in an indefinite sense are not usually written with figures.

Examples

- *The project will cost the government tens of millions.*
- *He addressed several thousand people.*
- *She answered hundreds of questions.*

but:

- *He spent about 30 hours on his trip report and had to wait nearly 15 days to be reimbursed for expenses.*

Indefinite Expressions Using Figures

Some numerical expressions may be required in certain contexts (such as a direct quotation) but are not recommended. Note that alternative wording is usually available.

Examples

- *100-odd* (better *more than 100*) *species of insects*
- *reserves of 50-plus* (better: *50 or more*) *vehicles*

Numerical Unit Modifiers

Numerical unit modifiers are written with hyphens.

Examples

- *third-level decision*
- *2-million-line network*
- *five-year plan*
- *20-kilometer* (or *20-km*) *march*
- *105-millimeter* (preferred *105-mm*) *guns*
- *eleventh-hour decision, four-hour delay*
- *7-meter* (never *7-m*) *limit*
- *10-room house, one- and two-bath apartments*
- *fourth-class hotel*
- *20th-century progress*
- *200-260-billion-ruble cost, 200-million-pound loan,*
  but *$200 million sale*
- *2-million-barrel-per-day* (or *2-million-b/d*) *output*
- *3-million-man Army*
- *a 1-cent increase*
- *6-percent increase, 6- to 7-percent* (or *6-to-7-percent*) *increase* (but *6 percent short*)
- *6-by-10-foot room* (but *20 to 30 feet long*—no hyphens if the unit of measure is plural)
- *late-1993 statistics*
- *10-month imprisonment*

Abbreviations of units of measure, including abbreviations formed by a single letter (such as *m* for *meter*), are acceptable in appropriate circumstances, such as in tables or in texts making frequent references to specific quantities. One exception, however, is a hyphenated modifier with a single-letter abbreviation, such as 7-m or 20-L. Spell them out (*7-meter*, *20-liter*) or change the unit of measure (*700-cm*, *20,000-mL*). Potentially confusing also are the abbreviations m^2 and m^3, which, although proper metric forms, could be mistaken for footnote references. Therefore, spell out *square meter(s)* or *cubic meter(s)*. *Sq m* and *cu m* may be used in a limited space. So may m^2 and m^3 if there is no possibility of ambiguity.

Numbers Close Together

When a cardinal number ordinarily given as a figure precedes a numerical unit modifier normally using a figure, consider rewording the sentence. Failing this, change one of the figures, preferably the smaller, up to 100, to a spelled-out word.

Examples

- *15 six-meter trees (or 15 trees 6 meters high)*
- *twelve 250-kilogram bombs (or 12 bombs each weighing 250 kilograms)*

Articles A, An

The rule on use of *a* or *an* also applies to numerical expressions and letter-number designators.

Examples

an 11-year-old   *a onetime winner*

an Su-20 Fitter aircraft   *a MiG-21 Fishbed*

Mixed Numbers

Avoid a combination of a whole number and a fraction by converting the fraction to a decimal quantity if possible.

Example

- *5.5 percent (or about 5.5 percent,* if a suggestion of precision is to be avoided*)*

In nonstatistical contexts, written-out phrases are preferred.

Examples

- *two and a half* (not one-half*) years ago*
- *two-and-a-half-year trial period* (better in some contexts: *30-month trial period*)

In statistical texts, however, precise reporting may require mixes of whole numbers and fractions.

References to Numbers as Numbers

Any number referred to as a number is given as a figure unless beginning a sentence.

Examples

- *The estimate could be off by a factor of 2 or 3.*
- *The data are rounded to the nearest 5.*
- *Divide by 5 to determine your share.*
- *His lucky number is 7.*

but:

- *Seven is his lucky number.* (If a number begins a sentence, spell it out or rephrase the sentence.)

References to Numbers in Nonliteral Sense

Numbers used in a metaphorical or figurative sense are spelled out without regard for the basic rules covering numbers above and below 10.

Examples

- *The Minister is famous for eleventh-hour decisions.*
- *Moreover, he is often a hundred-percent wrong.*
- *Because he is a shrewd politician he remains the number-two man in the regime instead of number twenty.*
- *There must be a thousand others who could run the Ministry better than he.*

Numbers in Tables and Graphics and for Pages, Paragraphs, and Footnotes

Such numbers, and sometimes those that immediately follow each bullet in a series that highlights quantities, are not subject to the general rules for numerals. Nor are numeral designators for tables, graphics, volumes, chapters, and other parts of publications. However, the text portions of footnotes and, unless space constraints dictate otherwise, of tables and graphics are governed by the same rules for numerals that are applicable to the text proper.

---

numerical compounds

Use a hyphen between the elements of compound numbers from 21 to 99 when they must be spelled out.

Examples

twenty-five	*one hundred twenty-one*
twenty-first	*one thousand three hundred twenty-one*
ninety-nine	

Use a hyphen in adjective compounds with a numerical first element.

Examples

- *two-sided question*
- *8-kilogram (*or *8-kg) turkey*
- *3-meter (*but never 3-m*) railing*
- *a 30-b/d increase*
- *six-room house*
- *the Six-Day War*
- *medium-to-high altitude*
- *medium-to-high-altitude interceptors*
- *Third Five-Year Plan*
- *18-year-old student*
- *24-hour period (*but *24 hours a day)*
- *10- to 20-year period (*or *10-to-20-year period)*
- *5-to-4 vote*
- *20th-century progress*
- *multimillion-dollar loan (*but *$20 million loan)*

Always use a hyphen between the elements of a fraction.

Examples

a two-thirds majority   *two-thirds of the legislature*

off	Should not be followed by *of* or *from*.
offput	Use *put off.*
one	When *one* is the subject, use a singular verb.

Example

- *One in every 10 US Senators is uncommitted.*

one-half, one-third	And the like are used when the fractions are precise. When precision is lacking, use a half, a third, and so forth.
only	Anchor *only* carefully to ensure that your meaning is clearly conveyed.

Examples

- *Only he attended the meeting.* (The others did not show up.)
- *He only attended the meeting.* (He did not make a speech.)
- *He attended only the meeting.* (He skipped the Happy Hour.)

Be sure that the *not only* and *but also* parts of the sentence are of parallel construction.

Examples

- *He is aware not only of the political consequences but also of the military dangers.*
- *He not only is aware of the political consequences but also recognizes the military dangers.*

opposition, opposed, opponent	*Opposition* takes the preposition *to*, as does *opposed; opponent* is followed by *of.*
organized bodies	**Government Bodies**

Capitalize the full proper name of a national government body as well as the shortened form of a proper name.

Examples

- *the British Parliament, the Parliament, Parliament (*but do not use parliamentarian*)*
- *the Argentine Congress, the Congress; the Ecuadorian Chamber of Deputies, the Chamber;* but *the Argentine legislature, the Ecuadorian legislature, the legislature*
- *the French Senate, the Senate, the upper house*
- *the Russian Council of Ministers, the Council of Ministers*

- *the British Cabinet, the Cabinet, the Liberal Democratic Cabinet, Cabinet member;* but *the Labor shadow cabinet* (This example does not apply across the board, especially if the term cabinet is used in reference to a body whose formal title does not resemble the English word. If in doubt, use lowercase.)
- *the Ministry of Economy, the Ministry; the Defense and Interior portfolios, proposed ministry of energy, the proposed ministry, various ministries, several ministries, the economic ministries, the foreign service, the civil service;* but *a Secret Service agent, the Defense and Interior portfolios, the Intelligence Community*
- *the Supreme Court*
- *the US Government, the Federal Government* (US only, also *Federal employee,* and so forth)*; the French Government, the French and Italian Governments, the Government of France, the Governments of France and Italy;* but *the government* (shortened form always lowercased)*; the federal government* (non-US, also *federal service,* and so forth)*, these governments, the Major government, the Tory government, the European governments; the executive, legislative, and judicial branches of government; the Clinton administration, the administration, the US administration, the Hashimoto administration.*

For a subnational government body, capitalize only the full proper name and avoid shortened forms that might be confused with national equivalents.

Example

- *the Maryland House of Delegates, the state legislature (*not the House*); the Quebec Parliament, the provincial parliament; the Jerusalem Municipal Council, the council, municipal councils all over Israel*

Organizations

Whenever possible, use the English translation, rather than the original language, in referring to the name of a foreign organization, institute, government body, political party, educational institution, corporation, or the like.

Often, however, there are compelling reasons—including convention, wide recognition, and untranslatability—for giving such a name in the original language. In such cases, do not italicize the name. If a translation is possible, relevant, or unobvious, supply one in parentheses following the foreign-language name. If appropriate, give instead or in addition an explanation of the name or description of the organization.

Examples

- *the joint Bulgarian-Hungarian building enterprise, Intransmech*
- *the Cuban news agency, Prensa Latina*
- *the Portuguese labor organization, Intersyndical*
- *the Lithuanian nationalist party, Sajudis*
- *the Tajik nationalist party, Vaadad*
- *the Ukrainian Popular Movement, Rukh*
- *the Buddhist organization Soka Gakkai and its political arm, Komeito*
- *chairperson of Yayasan Haropan Kita (Our Hope Foundation)*

- *the Wissenschaftrat (Science Council)*
- *the defunct an-Nahda (Renaissance) Party*
- *Hizballah, the Lebanese Shia group*
- *the Parti Quebecois*
- *photographed the Cathedral of Notre Dame*
- *graduate of the Sorbonne*
- *visited the al-Aqsa Mosque in Jerusalem*
- *vote of confidence in the Knesset (parliament)*
- *perpetrated by the Abu Nidal organization*

---

outside This is a preposition and should not be followed by of.

parallelism

To make the parallel clear, repeat a preposition, an article, the *to* of the infinitive, or the introductory word of a phrase or clause.

Example

- *Technology to boost production and to exploit natural resources . . .*

parameter, perimeter

Parameter is a legitimate word for mathematicians and other scientists, but it can be overused, as when *dimension* or *characteristic* would be just as good or better. Settle for *perimeter*—or *boundary* or *limit*—instead.

parentheses

Parentheses are used to set off a word, phrase, clause, or sentence that is inserted by way of comment or explanation within or after a sentence but that is structurally independent of it.

Examples

- *He graduated from Jefferson Teachers College (part of the state university system).*
- *Three old destroyers will be scrapped. (All three of them have been out of commission for some time.)*

Note that the placement of the periods above depends on whether the parenthetical insertion is part of the sentence that occasioned it or is an independent, complete sentence. In the following example, note that the comma follows the parentheses enclosing an insertion made in the middle of a series separated by commas.

Example

- *He visited Portland (Maine), Baltimore, and Dallas.*

Parentheses are used to enclose cross-references.

Examples

- *Japan's exports have risen steadily for the past 10 years (see figure 3).*
- *or . . . (annex A).*
- *or . . . (see inset).*
- or, as a separate sentence. *(See figure 3.)*

Parentheses are used to enclose numbers or letters in a series.

Example

- *We must set forth (1) our long-term goals, (2) our immediate objectives, and (3) the means at our disposal.* (Do not omit the first parenthesis in this usage.)

Use parentheses to enclose translations or explanations—if necessary—of foreign words or to enclose the original language following the English version.

Examples

- *He referred to the document as an estimate* (otsenka).
- *Her best known novel is* Aimez-vous Brahms? (Do You Like Brahms?). Italicize the translation because it is still a title.
- *Pointing to the skyline as we neared the capital, he trumpeted the nation's new* grandeza—*even as we passed one of the* favelas *(shantytowns) outside the city.*

---

parliament

Use only if it is the actual name of the body; otherwise, use *legislature* or the precise name (*National Assembly*, *Diet*, *Congress*)

---

parliamentarian

Is not an abbreviated form for a member of parliament. *Parliamentarians* are experts on parliamentary rules and procedures.

---

participles

Participles have the characteristics of both verbs and adjectives, so watch what they modify.

Example

- *Turning the corner, he found the view much changed.* (not: Turning the corner, the view was much changed.)

---

people, persons, personnel

The word *people* usually applies to sizable groups imprecisely enumerated, *persons* to smaller, usually explicit numbers.

Examples

- *Several thousand people showed up for the demonstration.*
- *Twenty persons were interviewed, nine persons were hired.*

Personnel is a collective noun (usually plural) referring to employees of an organization or to members of the armed services as a group. Do not use it as a substitute for *people* or *persons*.

---

percent

Numbers showing the relationship of a smaller to a larger quantity are frequently expressed in percentages. Figures are always used except at the beginning of a sentence that cannot be reworded. Do not abbreviate *percent* except to save space in tables or graphics, where the symbol (%) may be used.

Examples

- *The current plan projects a 20-percent increase by 1999.*
- *The party's share of seats rose 25 percent after the election.*
- *Five percent of the people polled . . .*

Be careful to distinguish between *percent* and *percentage point*. Percentage points (often shortened to *points*) are a commonly used measure of the difference between numbers expressed in percent.

Example

- *Inflation is expected to reach 13 percent this year, a full 3 percentage points higher than the 10-percent figure posted in 1995.*

For help with statistical techniques and methodological applications, contact OSS/Quantitative Methods Group.

period	The *period* is used at the end of a footnote, even if the note is not a structurally complete sentence. The *period* is not used: in annotations or legends on graphics, with item numbers in tables, to separate phrases in tables, or in table or text headings.
persons and organizations	Our authority for the spelling of names and titles of persons and organizations is OSS/KPG/Leadership Production Unit.
plural forms	May become singular when abbreviated.

Example

- *the Strategic Rocket Forces are (*but *the SRF is)*

plurality, majority	*Plurality* is not the same as *majority*. A group (or person) that receives more votes than any of three or more contenders, but less than 50 percent, has a *plurality*. A group (or person) receiving more than 50 percent has a *majority* and therefore a *plurality*. Neither term can be modified by "one-vote" or "one-seat."
political parties and other groups	Capitalize the full or shortened name of a political party, but do not capitalize the word *party* standing alone.

Examples

- *the Italian Socialist Party, the Socialist Party, the PSI*
- *the Christian Democratic Union, the party, the CDU*
- *the British (*or *Australian,* or *New Zealand) Labor Party, the party, Labor (*as in *Labor's chances in the election)*
- *Israel's Likud bloc*
- *the Palestine Liberation Organization, the PLO*
- *the Abu Nidal organization*
- *the 26th Party Congress,* but *a recent party congress*

political philosophies	**Communism** Capitalize the words *Communist* and *Communism* when referring to any part, adherent, or aspect of the Communist movement, whether referring to a form

of government, a nonruling party, or even a Communist party that does not have one of these words in its name. Most derivatives, including the opposites, of these words also have a capital *C*.

Examples

- *ruling Communist party or parties*
- *the Communist countries*
- *a non-Communist country*
- *a Communist ruling party called the Socialist Unity Party*
- *a Communist opposition party called the People's Party*
- *conference of European Communist parties*
- *anti-Communist movement*
- *a group dedicated to anti-Communism*
- *a pro-Communist organization*
- *pre-Communist China*

but:

- *Eurocommunism*

Communist Jargon

The Communist countries and parties often call themselves *"Socialist"* or *"socialist."* In paraphrasing Communist statements, put such references in quotation marks. The same applies to *imperialism* and *imperialist* (and to *anti-imperialism* and *anti-imperialist).*

Non-Communist Philosophies

Capitalize in accordance with the parties' own names the words referring to members of organized parties, but do not capitalize words referring to non-Communist political philosophies and their adherents.

Examples

- *a Socialist, a Liberal, a Laborite, a Conservative, a Tory, a Social Christian, a Christian Socialist* (all party members)
- *A British socialist is likely to be a member of the Labor Party.*
- *The insurgent nationalists are hoping for support from one of the Communist states.*
- *The socialist parties of Western Europe include the British Labor Party.*

An exception is made for Christian Democracy (and for Christian Democrat and Christian Democratic).

---

political subdivisions

As a general rule, do not abbreviate the names of political subdivisions such as provinces, departments, or states (US or foreign). Abbreviation of states of the United States or provinces of Canada is acceptable if the names are used repeatedly to distinguish cities of the same names in different jurisdictions. Most of the time there is no need to use abbreviations of political subdivisions for well-known cities such as *Toronto, Vancouver, New York,* and *Washington* (the DC is almost never necessary in intelligence contexts). Do distinguish *London, Ontario*, from *London, England*.

It is not necessary to put the name of the country after that of any well-known city (*Bern, Islamabad, Canberra, Brasilia*). Use country names with cities not well known.

---

practical, practicable

Practical connotes useful and should be differentiated from *practicable*, which means capable of being carried out in action.

Examples
- *It was practicable to build a highway* (it could be done).
- *It was not practical* (because it would receive little use).

---

precipitate, precipitately, precipitant, precipitous

Precipitate and *precipitately* apply to rash or hasty human actions. *Precipitant* and its adverb are used in the same general sense, but with stress on rushing or falling headlong. *Precipitous* refers to physical steepness.

---

preclude, prevent

Generally, *prevent* applies to persons as its object, *preclude* to events.

Examples
- *The bad weather prevents me from leaving today.*
- *The bad weather precludes a departure today.*

---

prefixes and suffixes

Unhyphenated

Do not insert a hyphen after a prefix joined to a solid (unhyphenated, one-word) compound.

Examples

antigunrunning	*postreentry*
nonlifelike	*submachinegun*
nonoceangoing	*ultrarightwing*

Prefixes and suffixes other than those listed below usually form a solid compound with a noncapitalized word.

Examples, Prefixes

afterhours	*counterintelligence*	*semiofficial*
antedate	*hydroelectric*	*subcommittee*
antiaircraft	*multicolor*	*transship*
biweekly	*nonferrous*	*ultramodern*
byproduct	*predetente*	*unofficial*

Examples, Suffixes

clockwise	*lifelike*	*partnership*
fourfold	*northward*	

Hyphenated

Hyphenate words with the prefixes *ex-, self-, quasi-,* and *vice-* and suffixes *-free, -designate,* and *-elect.* Hyphenate the prefix *pro-* when it means favoring. These hyphenated compounds retain their hyphens in the predicate form.

Examples, Prefixes

ex-governor	*pro-oligarchy*	*self-interest*
ex-serviceman	*quasi-academic*	*vice-chairmanship* (but
pro-democratic	*quasi-public*	*vice chair)*
pro-life	*self-control*	*vice-president-elect*

Examples, Suffixes

councilor-elect	*President-elect Jones*
minister-designate	*rent-free*

Except after the short prefixes *co, de, pre,* and *re,* which are generally written solid, a hyphen is used to avoid doubling a vowel when adding a prefix or tripling a consonant when adding a suffix.

Examples, Prefixes

cooperation	*overreact*	*reestablishment*
deemphasize	*posttreatment*	*subbasement*
nonnuclear	*preexisting*	
but:		
anti-inflation	*semi-independent*	*ultra-atomic*

Examples, Suffixes

hull-less	*shell-like*

Prefixing a Hyphenated Compound

Use a hyphen to join a prefix to an already hyphenated compound.

Examples

pre-cease-fire talks	*pseudo-peace-loving group*

A hyphen is used with a prefix normally forming solid compounds if omission of the hyphen would lead to mispronunciation or cause confusion with a word spelled identically but without a hyphen.

Examples

*co-op (*but *cooperative)*	*re-cover* (cover again)
mid-ice, under-ice	*re-create* (create again)
mini-estates	*re-form* (form again)
multi-ply (several plies)	*re-present* (present again)
pre-position (position in advance)	*re-treat* (treat again)
pro-state	*un-ionized*
pro-war	

A hyphen is used to join duplicated prefixes.

Examples

counter-countermeasures	*sub-subcommittee*

A hyphen (unless an en dash is called for) is used to join a prefix or a suffix in a compound with a capitalized word.

Examples

Africa-wide	*pre-Renaissance*
anti-Castro	*pro-British*
neo-Nazi	*Kennedy-like*
non-Communist	*un-American*
exceptions:	
nonMIRVed	*unMIRVed*

En dash called for

Latin America–wide	*pre–World War II*

Retain the hyphen if it is part of an established formal name.

Examples

Nuclear Non-Proliferation Treaty	*Multi-Fiber Arrangement*

A prefix (except un) normally forming a solid compound is often followed by a hyphen when joined with a two-word or hyphenated compound to form a unit modifier.

Examples

anti-guided-missile	*post-civil-war*
anti-submarine-warfare	*post-target-tracking*
ex-civil-servant	*pre-martial-law*
non-missile-equipped	*pro-arms-control*
non-nuclear-powered	*semi-land-mobile*
but:	
antiballistic missile	*uncalled-for*
antiradiation-homing	*unself-conscious*

For many of the previous terms, rephrasing the sentence might be a better solution than insertion of the extra hyphen.

Examples
- *defense against guided missiles* (instead of *anti-guided-missile defense*)
- *aircraft not equipped with missiles* (instead of *non-missile-equipped aircraft*)
- *a system that is partially land mobile* (instead of *a semi-land-mobile system*)

prepositions	The rule that *prepositions* must never come at the ends of sentences no longer applies.

presently	Means in a short time; do not use it to mean at present, currently, or now.

principal, principle, principled	*Principal* is an adjective meaning most important, or a noun referring to a leader or to money. *Principle* is a noun only. It means basic truth, rule of conduct, fundamental law; *principled* is its related adjective.

prior to, before

Prior to is appropriate when a notion of requirement is involved.

Example
- *The law must be passed prior to 1 July.*

Otherwise, *before* is the better word.

pristine

Describes something that is in its original condition, or primitive. *Pristine* should not be used as a synonym for new or clean.

probable, possible

Analysts, particularly military analysts, are tempted to use probable or possible when *what probably is* or *what possibly is* is the proper formulation.

Example
- *The attache saw what probably is a missile.* (Not: The attache saw a probable missile—could the officer have seen an improbable [or impossible] missile?)

proliferator, proliferating

The noun *proliferator* describes a country engaged in unwarranted dissemination of nuclear weapon technology and capability. The complementary adjective is *proliferating*.

proper names

Capitalize a common noun when it forms part of a proper name. However, do not use capitalization as a substitute for the name of the place or thing or when it becomes separated from the rest of the name by an intervening word or phrase.

Examples

* *Social Democratic Party, the party*
* *Catholic Church, the church*
* *Howard University, the university*
* *Quebec Province, Province of Quebec; the province; Quebec, Canada's separatist province*

This rule does not apply to certain well-known short forms of specific proper names.

Examples

* *the British Commonwealth, the Commonwealth*
* *the Panama (or Suez) Canal, the Canal*
* *the Golan Heights, the Heights*
* *the English Channel, the Channel*
* *the Persian Gulf, the Gulf*
* *the Horn of Africa, the Horn*
* *the Korean Peninsula, the Peninsula*
* *the Olympic Games, the Games, the Olympics, the Winter Olympics*

A noun common to two or more proper names is capitalized in the plural form when preceded by the proper adjectives in those names.

Examples

* *Montgomery and Fairfax Counties*
* *Georgetown and George Washington Universities*
* *Baltic and Black Seas*

Derivatives of Proper Names

Do not capitalize derivatives of proper names used with acquired independent meanings.

Examples

anglicized words	*italic type*
byzantine organization	*pasteurized milk*
diesel engine	*roman type*
draconian measures	*venetian blinds*
exceptions:	
Castroite sympathies	*Marxist, Leninist*
degrees Fahrenheit	*Molotov cocktail*
Francophone	*Morse code*
Gaullist policies	*neo-Stalinism, de-Stalinization*
Islamization	

Particles in Proper Names

Capitalize the definite article, or its equivalent in a foreign language, when it is part of an official name. When such a name is used adjectively, an uncapitalized *the* might be used and, despite the redundancy, would precede a capitalized non-English equivalent.

Examples

- *The Hague,* but *the Second Hague Conference*
- *El Salvador,* but *the El Salvador situation*
- *The Bahamas,* but *the Bahamas Tourist Office*
- *The Gambia,* but *the Gambia mapping project*

For some country names the definite article is used but is not capitalized because it is not part of the official name (for example, *the United Kingdom, the United States, the Vatican*) or because the convention has been to use a lowercase *t.* Guidance on country names and on the nouns and adjectives denoting nationality is given in *The World Factbook,* produced by OSS/KPG/World Factbook Staff.

Example

- *the Philippines* (the proper adjective is *Philippine;* the people are called *Filipinos*)

Do not omit the article before a country name in a series if the article is used when the name stands alone.

Example

- *the United States and the United Kingdom* (not the United States and United Kingdom)

There is no *the* in *Congo, Cote d'Ivoire, Seychelles, Sudan, Ukraine,* or *Western Sahara.*

In certain personal names, particles such as *d', de, den, du, van,* and *von* are usually not capitalized unless they begin a sentence.

Examples

- *. . . achieved independence while de Gaulle was President. De Gaulle, however, did . . .*
- *. . opposed by the den Uyl government. Den Uyl's policy differs from that of van Agt in . . .*

In other names, particles are often dropped when the family name alone is used.

Example

- *Mohammad Zia-ul-Haq,* but *the late General Zia*

Anglicized versions of foreign names vary in the matter of retaining or dropping particles and in the use of capital letters. In any case, the preference of the person named, if known, should be followed. Our authority for the spelling of personal names is OSS/KPG/Leadership Production Unit.

Installations

After a specific installation name has been established in a report, a distinctive part of it may be combined with a generic noun to form a shortened proper name, which should be capitalized.

Examples

- *Odesa Tractor Plant 76* (full), *Odesa Plant 76* (short)
- *St. Petersburg SS-19 ICBM Complex Mobile Base 3* (full), *St. Petersburg Mobile ICBM Base 3* (short)

The place name and generic name, however, do not qualify as a short proper name because facilities of the same general type (such as a plant or barracks) may be nearby or similarly named facilities may be located elsewhere.

Examples

- *Odesa plant* (several plants may be located in Odesa)
- *mobile ICBM base 3* (many bases have this designator)

---

proper nouns

Do not use a hyphen in a compound proper noun or in a capitalized coined name used as a unit modifier, in either its basic or derived form.

Examples

Cold War tensions	*Latin American states*
French Revolutionary period	*Third World countries*
Intelligence Community Staff	*World War II period*

But the hyphen is used if the proper noun is normally a combined form.

Examples

Hispanic-American culture	*French-English descent*

This rule does not apply to numerical compounds in an expression such as *Fifth Five-Year Plan*, nor would it apply entirely in an expression incorporating an already hyphenated coined name (*Six-Day War euphoria*).

protagonist	The leading or principal character, not necessarily a champion of an idea or course of action. Chief protagonist is redundant.
provided	In the sense of *if*, *provided* is preferable to providing.
punctuation	The purpose of punctuation is to make writing clear. Punctuation is based on meaning, grammar, syntax, and custom. The trend for formal writing should always be toward less punctuation, not more. Less punctuation does, however, call for skillful phrasing to avoid ambiguity and to ensure exact interpretation.

The general principles governing the use of punctuation are:

1. If it does not clarify the text it should be omitted.

2. In the choice and placing of punctuation marks the sole aim should be to bring out more clearly the author's thought. Punctuation should aid in reading and prevent misreading.

The *GPO Style Manual*, the *Merriam Webster's New Collegiate Dictionary*, and *The Chicago Manual of Style* explain and illustrate rules of punctuation that are applicable to intelligence reports.

qualifiers

Do not weaken judgments supported by direct evidence by inserting words like *apparently, evidently, seemingly, purportedly*. Conversely, you cannot strengthen judgments based on weak evidence by words like *obviously, undoubtedly, clearly*.

quality control for publications

The five most common problems that are discovered at the last minute:

1. Incorrect pagination.

2. Table of contents that does not match the text.

3. Incorrectly numbered graphics or tables.

4. A typo in a running head.

5. A typo on the cover or the title page.

Checklist

Check pagination.

Check the table of contents against the text (titles, page numbers).

Check running heads and feet (spelling, consistency, typeface, appropriate wording). Check the publication number, tracking number, and classification-block information.

Check text subheadings (consistent format, spelling) and at least the first sentence under each.

Check tables, photos, graphs, maps, and insets:
• Placement in text and figure numbers.
• Legend and footnotes.
• Format consistency.
• Table column alignment.

Check that footnotes (numbering, callouts) are correct.

Read word for word any preface, key judgments, summary, conclusions, or recommendations sections.

Read transitions (from column to column, page to page) to look for dropped or duplicated text.

Skim each page:

- Check all cross-references (be sure you have filled in placeholders for page numbers and so forth).
- Check sequence (alphabetical, numerical) in all lists.
- Check for pairs (parentheses, brackets, quotation marks, dashes).
- Check margins and word divisions.

Check wherever errors have been corrected.

---

question mark

Apart from its principal function of terminating interrogative sentences, the question mark is used to show the writer's uncertainty (or ignorance), as when it is placed next to (or instead of) a figure in a tabulation. Similar application can be made within the text, but this should be kept to a minimum.

Example

- *The paper was a hodgepodge, trying to deal with poets as diverse as Omar Khayyam (? -1132?) and Geoffrey Chaucer (1340?-1400).*

---

quotation marks

Single quotation marks never appear in American usage unless double quotation marks are present. Quotation marks, single or double, must always be used in a pair.

Double Quotation Marks

A pair of double quotation marks is used to enclose direct quotations.

Examples

- *"The President," he said, "will veto the bill."*
- *Who asked, "Why?"*
- *Why label it a "gentlemen's agreement"?*
- *The citation read: "For meritorious service beyond the call of duty."*

If the quotation is a long one—about half a dozen lines or more—set it off by indentation of 1 pica on each side within the text column, omitting the quotation marks.

Use quotation marks to set off titles of poems and songs and of articles, short stories, and other parts of a longer work.

Examples

- *"Hallelujah" is the best known chorus from Handel's* Messiah.
- *Who wrote the article "Second Looks" in that issue of* PC Magazine*?*
- *Have you read Robert Frost's poem "Fire and Ice"?*

Quotation marks are used to set off words or phrases used or cited in a special sense. (In this function, quotation marks are sometimes used interchangeably with italic type. Italic type generally is used for cited letters and words, and quotation marks to enclose phrases or clauses used as examples.)

Examples

- *Do not capitalize the* s *in* socialist *in the phrase "most British socialists join the Labor Party."*
- *The North Korean press put the blame on "US imperialism."*
- *If this is a "working" vacation, why are you lying there doing nothing?*

Be careful not to overuse or misuse quotation marks—or italic type. Use them to enclose words used in a special sense (such as Communist jargon) but do not use quotation marks to apologize for acceptable English words or in an attempt to redeem slang. And never allow the reader to wonder why they were used. The reader may assume that the quotation marks connote some "special" meaning, and he may waste time looking for an explanation.

Single Quotation Marks

A pair of single quotation marks is used to enclose a quotation within a quotation. Exception: if a quotation is set off by indentation, rather than by quotation marks, a quotation within it would use double, not single, quotation marks.

Punctuation With Quotation Marks

Commas and periods always go inside quotation marks (single or double). Semicolons and colons always go outside the final quotation mark. Other punctuation marks are placed inside quotation marks at the end of a sentence only if they are part of the matter quoted.

Examples

- *He said, "I used the term 'gentlemen's agreement.'"*
- *He asked, "Why label it a 'gentlemen's agreement'?"*
- *"Remember," she said, "what Grandfather used to advise: 'When other people run, you walk.'"*

Terms Precluding Need for Quotation Marks

Quotation marks are usually not necessary to enclose expressions following terms such as *known as, called*, or *so-called*.

Examples

- *Aluminum is known as aluminium in Canada.*
- *Your so-called investigating body has not done much investigating.*
- *If this is called profit and loss, when do we start profiting?*

They may be used even here, however, to give special emphasis to the quoted or verbatim nature of the expression given, especially if sarcasm or bad grammar is involved.

Example

• *He criticized what he called the "looks funny" school of editing.*

Other such terms—*entitled, named, endorsed,* and *signed,* or their equivalent—call for either italicizing or enclosing in quotation marks the word or words that follow them.

Examples

• *The card was signed "You know who."*
• *He was named "chief cook and bottle washer" by his housemates.*
• *The word* radar *is an acronym derived from the term "radio detecting and ranging."*

Craft

Do not use quotation marks or italic type for the names of ships, aircraft, or spacecraft. Craft is both singular and plural in reference to a plane or boat.

Unit Modifiers

Do not use a hyphen in a unit modifier enclosed in quotation marks unless it is normally a hyphenated form, and do not use quotation marks in lieu of hyphens.

Examples

• *a "spare the rod" approach to parenthood*
• *the "one-man woman" plots of many operas*

ratios, odds, scores, returns	Use numbers for each of these numerical situations.

Examples

- *Women were outnumbered 17 to 1.*
- *The doctor-to-patient ratio was 1:17.*
- *He had a 50-50 chance of winning.*
- *The Irish won, 21 to 6.* (Note the use of the comma.)
- *The first vote gave the Democrats 21 seats, the Socialists 9, and the Communists 5.*
- *The measure was approved by a 90-to-3 vote.*
- *a 3-to-1 advantage*

but:

- *current assets/current liabilities ratio* |
| **ranges of numbers below the millions** | Except in ranges of years, and page or paragraph references, avoid hyphens in ranges of numbers below the millions in order to prevent misreading. Use prepositions and conjunctions instead.

Examples

- *The march covered 10 to 15 kilometers* (not 10-15 kilometers).
- *The league membership is between 15,000 and 20,000* (Never use combinations of prepositions and hyphens such as between 15,000-20,000 to express a complete range of values below the millions.)
- *Model numbers 847,312 through 873,214 have been recalled* (not from 847,312-873,214).

In tabular material, especially where space limitations apply, the use of hyphens in ranges of numbers is acceptable. |
| **ranges of numbers in the millions** | Hyphens are acceptable (although not required usage) in ranges of numbers in the millions and multimillions.

Examples

- *Natural gas reserves are estimated at 20-30 billion cubic feet.*
- *Production rose to 2.0-3.5 million tons annually during the period 1996-97.*
- *The range of estimated construction costs has increased from $500-600 million to $2-3 billion.* (Do not repeat the dollar sign in ranges like these. Do not write $500 to $600 million or $2 to $3 billion. Writing $500 million to $600 million or $2 billion to $3 billion is correct but would be awkward.)
- *by about 2-2.5 million*
- *from 1.6-2.1 million* |

reason	After an opening like *the reason for,* the clause containing the reason should begin with *that,* not because or why.

Example

- *The reason for his failure was that he was ill. (Better: He failed because he was ill.)*

---

redound, rebound	*Redound* means to have an effect.

Example

- *The plan redounds to his credit.*

Rebound means to bounce back.

Example

- *The economy rebounded last month.*

---

redundancies	Phrases that succumb to repetition. Below are selected redundancies.

Examples

accidentally misfired	*first-ever*
adequate enough	*foreign imports*
advance reservation	*free gift*
as has been mentioned previously	*future potential*
as was noted before	*future prospects*
both agree	*future successor*
build a new house	*good chance*
bureaucratic redtape	*historical monuments*
chief mainstay	*historical past*
church seminarians	*holy shrine*
close confidant	*in close proximity*
close personal friend	*interact together*
combine together	*joint coalition*
completely surrounded	*lag behind*
consensus of opinion	*little booklet*
could possibly	*live studio audience*
current status	*long litany*
established tradition	*major crisis*
exact same	*major milestone*
exile abroad	*meet personally*
exports beyond their border	*military troops*
eyewitness at the scene	*mutual cooperation*
final vestiges	*naval marines*
first began	*old adage*

own personal	*still continues*
particularly pronounced	*still remains*
past custom	*still retains*
personal autograph	*sufficient enough*
personal charisma	*sum total*
piecemeal on a piece basis	*tandem couple*
professional career	*temporary respite*
rally together	*temporary suspension*
real possibility	*thin veneer*
relocate elsewhere	*top business magnate*
separate isolation cells	*true facts*
separate out	*trusted confidant*
share together	*underlying premise*
single greatest, single most	*unexpected surprise*
small cottage	*unite together*
small village	*well-known reputation*
sound logic	*young baby*

regime

Has a disparaging connotation and should not be used when referring to democratically elected governments or, generally, to governments friendly to the United States.

relations, ties, links

Relations should be followed by the preposition *with*.

Example

• *This country is about to establish relations with that one.*

Ties (or *links*) should be followed by *to*.

Example

• *That country has ties (links) to this one.*

relatively, comparatively

Should be used only when the intended comparison can be easily grasped.

Example

• *He has a relatively heavy workload.* (Relative to what? Last year? Last week?)

relevant, important

Relevant refers to something that has a bearing on the matter at hand and should be followed by *to*.

Example

• *His speech was relevant to the problem.*

Do not use relevant when you mean *important*.

---

religious terms

Capitalize the names of religions, religious bodies, and the terms for their adherents and writings.

Examples

Allah	*God*
an Episcopalian	*Islam*
a Jew	*Judaism*
a Muslim	*the Koran*
a Protestant	*Koranic law*
the Bible	*Prophet (Muhammad)*
Biblical text	*Russian Orthodoxy*
Buddha	*Sabbath*
Catholicism	*Semite, Semitism*
Christianity	*the Talmud*
Dalai Lama	*Talmudic scholar*

Do not capitalize such terms when they are used in a nonreligious sense.

Example

• *This style guide attempts to be catholic in its approach to English usage.*

Religious Leaders

The terms for and titles of religious leaders are capitalized preceding a name and occasionally are capitalized following the name or when used alone.

Examples

• *Archbishop Glemp . . . the Archbishop;* but *appointment of an archbishop* (in a political context simply use the name for subsequent references . . . *meetings between Glemp and the authorities*)
• *Pope John Paul II . . . the Pope;* but *election of a pope; future popes; papal, papacy*

---

represent

Means to depict or symbolize, not constitute.

Examples

• *The red line on the map represents the boundary between France and Germany.* (not: *South African gold represents most of the world's output.*)

---

reveal, expose, disclose, divulge

Reveal implies an unveiling of something not previously known; *expose* refers to the making public of something reprehensible; *disclose* refers to making public something that has been private; *divulge* refers to making public something that has been secret.

SALT, START, MBFR, INF	Sometimes an abbreviation not ending in *s* stands for a plural term, as in *SALT* (strategic arms limitation talks) and *START* (strategic arms reduction talks). Note that uppercase is not used in spelling out these terms. The abbreviation *SAL* (strategic arms limitation) is also used. The negotiating rounds at Geneva in the 1970s have generally been abbreviated *SALT I* and *SALT II*. Note that it is redundant to write "START talks" or "SALT talks." This is not the case with *MBFR talks*, in which the abbreviation covers only the purpose of the talks—mutual and balanced force reduction. The same logic applies to *INF talks*—negotiations concerning intermediate-range nuclear forces. It is customary not to use an article with these abbreviations (Russian position on SALT . . . on MBFR . . . on START . . . on INF). A further word on START and SALT: although the terms they stand for are plural, the abbreviations are construed as singular.

sanction	As a noun, *sanction* has meanings that are almost in opposition: from approval and encouragement to penalty and coercion. It should therefore be used only when the context makes its meaning clear. As a verb, *sanction* picks up only the approval aspect of the noun.

scientific notation	A scientific and technical paper may require exponential expression of quantities in the multimillions: $10^{17} \, watts/cm^2$.

seasons	Do not capitalize *spring, summer, fall* (*autumn*), or *winter*. As a general rule, use the definite article in referring to a season and use *of* before the year.

Examples
* *in the fall of 1992*
but:
* *her fall 1992 election triumph*

Do not use seasonal references in writing about the Southern Hemisphere, where seasons occur six months before/after they do above the Equator. If it is necessary to mention the season in a Southern Hemisphere context, be sure your meaning is clear.

Examples
* *The Argentine naval exercise took place in the harsh sea conditions of last July's austral winter.*
* *The party's chances in the February byelection will probably be helped by the expected low voter turnout during Sydney's peak summer vacation season.*

semicolon

The *semicolon* can be regarded to some extent as a supercomma because it supersedes the comma in cases where a comma is not clear enough for the function intended.

The semicolon is used between coordinate elements containing commas. If such a series is in midsentence, reword the sentence to put the series at the end.

Examples

- *The major inputs are iron ore, which comes from Poland; nitric acid, which is imported from the Czech Republic; magnesium, which is supplied primarily by Russia; and nickel, which is furnished in adequate quantities by domestic producers.*
- *The principal legatees were a niece, Jane Wilson; a longtime servant, Samuel Jones; and the city library.*

The semicolon is used to separate the clauses of a compound sentence when a coordinating conjunction (*and, but, or, nor, so, yet*) is not used.

Examples

- *She received a B.A. degree from Notre Dame in 1993; later she attended the University of Virginia.*
- *A fool babbles continuously; a wise man holds his tongue.*

A semicolon is used before an independent second clause introduced by one of the conjunctive adverbs (*accordingly, also, consequently, furthermore, hence, however, indeed, moreover, nevertheless, otherwise, so, still, then, therefore, thus, yet*).

Examples

- *Some Americans spend millions of dollars for junk food; consequently, their teeth are rapidly deteriorating.*
- *William speaks English, French, German, and Russian well; moreover, he understands Persian, Urdu, and Vietnamese.*
- *You should take your umbrella with you; otherwise, you are likely to get wet.*

The semicolon is used to separate phrases in tabular columns of comments or extended descriptions.

shall, will

(Past forms *should* and *would*.) In the first person, *shall* denotes simple futurity; in the second and third persons, *shall* denotes promise, inevitability, command, or compulsion. *Will* is the other way around. In our publications, *will* will do.

sherpa, sous-sherpa	A sherpa is the personal representative of a G-7 head of government, responsible for preparing that leader for the now-annual G-7 summits. Sherpas are also engaged in support for P-8 meetings (G-7 plus Russia on political issues). They meet frequently with their counterparts to work out the summit agenda as well as positions and other summit details. One of several assistants to the G-7 sherpa is the *sous-sherpa*; countries generally have economic and finance sherpas; political issues are handled by the countries' political directors who are not, strictly speaking, sous-sherpas but are, in effect, members of the country's sherpa team.
should, will probably	Use *will probably* in presenting intelligence judgments.
slash	The *slash* (also called *diagonal*, *oblique*, *shill*, *slant*, *solidus*, and *virgule*) should be used sparingly and never in place of a hyphen or dash.

The slash is used to indicate a 12-month period occurring in two calendar years.

Examples

fiscal year 1995/96 *marketing year 1994/95*
crop year 1993/94 *academic year 1996/97*

The slash is used to represent *per* in abbreviations.

Examples

km/h (kilometers per hour) *r/min* (revolutions per minute)

The slash is used to separate alternatives.

Examples

- *These designs are intended for high-heat and/or high-speed applications.* (Try to substitute *and* or *or* for *and/or*. In this example *and* alone would suffice. In the ensuing one *or* could replace the slash with no confusion of meaning.)
- *He sat for hours at his PC in a catatonic/frenzied trance trying to cover every possible contingency.*

The slash is used to indicate combination in certain instances.

Examples

- *Community support was pivotal for this Japanese/US-backed proposal.* (Use of an en dash or another hyphen is awkward.)
- *Insurgent forces were armed with Cuban/Russian-supplied weapons.* (Use of a slash here could indicate either a combination or alternatives, the latter reflecting Moscow's practice of sometimes using surrogates to supply its clients.)
- *The goal of one-man/one-vote was never forgotten. They campaigned on a one-man/one-vote platform.* (Keep the hyphen and slash whether a noun form or an adjective form.)
- *The group endorsed the Christian Democratic Union/Christian Social Union platform.*
- *the T-54/55 tanks*

snowflakes	Used in biographic summaries. ***Example*** • *Age 82 . . . retired in 1990 . . . probably responsible for S&T.*
species	Lowercase. ***Example*** • *sapiens*
spelling	Use the lists in this Style Guide first, then use the *GPO Style Manual*, then the current edition of *Merriam-Webster's New Collegiate Dictionary*. For geographic terms, the cartographers in OSS/MPG/Cartography Center are the authority. For personal names, contact OSS/KPG/Leadership Production Unit.
statistics	For help with statistical techniques and methodological applications, contact OSS/Quantitative Methods Group.
stealth	Referring to aircraft with low radar signatures and to its technology, *stealth* is written in lowercase. ***Examples*** *the stealth bomber* *stealth technology* *counterstealth*
strategy, tactics	*Strategy* is an overall plan of action, usually military action; *tactics* are specific plans or maneuvers designed to advance strategic goals. Nuclear weapons can be included in both strategic and tactical planning.
subjective words	Subjective words like *fortunately, unfortunately,* and *naturally* may suggest that the analyst is biased. Likewise, *negative trends, negative impressions, negative actions* can suggest a lack of evenhandedness.
subjunctive	The subjunctive mood is used most commonly to describe conditions contrary to fact. *If he were* is preferred to if he was, but use it sparingly.

table	As a verb, *table* can mean to put a bill aside. In British use, *table* can also mean to introduce a bill for consideration. Use the word only when the meaning is unmistakable.
technical terms	The jargon should be in "lay" English, unless you are confident that a technical word or phrase will be easily understood by the general reader.
Tel Aviv	Do not use Tel Aviv as a stand-in for Israel or for the Israeli Government.
that, which	*That* introduces a restrictive clause—a phrase that is essential to the meaning or structure of the sentence.

that, which (continued)

Example

• *The car that ran the traffic light was a Ford.* (Identifies the car.)

Which introduces a nonrestrictive clause—a phrase that is unessential but adds information. Nonrestrictive clauses are preceded and followed by commas.

Example

• *The car, which ran the traffic light, was a Ford.* (Describes the car.)

there	Try to avoid using *there is* or *there are* to start a sentence. When you must lead off with a *there is* construction, be sure the number of the verb agrees with the subject that follows.

Examples

• *An artillery regiment is on the border* (better than: There is an artillery regiment on the border).
• *There are a headquarters building for each unit and numerous other structures.*

this	Often used as a demonstrative pronoun, representing in a single word a situation or a thought expressed earlier. If *this* finds itself without a clear antecedent, either rework the sentence to make the antecedent unmistakable (proximity is the best solution) or add the appropriate word or words after *this*.
thousands	Numbers with more than three digits are written with commas, except for years, radiofrequencies, military unit designators, clock time, most serial numbers, and the fractional portions of decimal numbers.

Examples

- *A force of 20,000 (*never 20 thousand*) troops was needed.*
- *She had traveled 6,187 kilometers as of 1400 hours.*
- *The exact weight is 3,399.243046 grams.*
- *The station operated on a frequency of 1800 kHz.*
- *He was assigned to the 1028th Brigade.*
- *He picked up job number 518225 10-88.*

but:

- *one hundred seventy-two thousand*

---

thus

Never use thusly.

---

time

Clock Time

The time of day is written in the 24-hour system, without internal punctuation.

Examples

- *The managers met at 0745 hours.*
- *The satellite was launched at 1800 EDT (2400 GMT).*
- *The midday break is 1300-1430.*

Other Time Expressions

Apart from the situations covered above, references to time follow the basic rules for numbers above and below 10.

Examples

- *The protest lasted for eight days.*
- *Payment is acceptable on the 29th day after the due date.*

---

times phrases

Numbers showing the relationship of a larger quantity to a smaller one are often accompanied by the word *times* and, unless decimals are used, are governed by the basic rules for numbers on either side of 10.

Examples

five times as large   *10 times greater*   *2.5 times more powerful*

Various ways of expressing (or not expressing) proportion with the word *times* are shown below. Sometimes the message is clearer if expressed in percent. One can also use the suffix *fold*, but this is somewhat awkward when decimal factors are involved.

Examples

- *The number of tanks increased to five times the prewar level.* (This is a 400-percent, or fourfold, increase.)

- *The number of tanks increased five times.* (There were five increases in the number of tanks.)
- *There are five times as many tanks as there were before the war.* (The present number is 400 percent, or four times, greater than the prewar number; is five times the prewar number; and has undergone a fourfold increase.)

If the suffix *fold* is attached to a whole number written solid and unhyphenated, spell the resulting word without a hyphen.

Examples

fourfold	*twentyfold*
tenfold	*hundredfold*

Otherwise use a figure and a hyphen.

Examples

6-fold	*21-fold*

The principal advantage of *fold* is that it sometimes permits a more precise translation of data reported in a foreign (particularly Slavic) language. A 5.75-fold increase, however, can just as easily be expressed as a 575-percent increase, or an increase to 6.75 times the previous level.

Never use meaningless expressions such as "four times smaller," which sometimes is written by an author who means to say "one-fourth as large." If in doubt, contact OSS/Quantitative Methods Group.

---

time zones

Almost always lowercase.

Examples

central standard	*eastern daylight*
but:	
Pacific standard	*Zulu time*

---

titles of persons

Before the Name

Capitalize any valid title (or short form of it) immediately preceding a person's name. Use the highest title, not the highest title followed by a military rank. The plural form of the title preceding more than one name is also capitalized. In front of a title, the prefix *ex-* and the adjectives *former* and *then* are not capitalized, nor are the suffixes *-designate* and *-elect*. Do not confuse a mere description with a title by capitalizing it.

Examples

- *President Gligorov, Acting President Powell, Foreign Minister Bostwick, First Deputy Premier Smith*
- *People's Deputy Yarin, Senator Gonzalez*

- *PLO Chief/Chairman Arafat*
- *Prime Ministers Major and Chretien*
- *Bishop Jones, Prof. Mary Brown, Professor Brown*
- *Mayor Black, Assistant Principal Jones*
- *party General Secretary Gorbachev,* but *party secretary Chebrikov and Politburo candidate member Maslyukov (*examples unique to the Communist world*)*
- *second secretary Ligachev* (this is not the actual title in Russia, but Second Secretary is the title in the republics)
- *party Secretary Craxi* (uppercase any party top leader's formal title preceding the name), *ruling-party Chairman Jones*
- *Chief Justice Ramirez, Associate Justice Williams, Justices Ramirez and Williams*
- *former Prime Minister Callaghan, then Defense Minister Sharon, ex-President Echeverria, ex–Foreign Minister Gromyko, Prime Minister–designate Peres, President-elect Salinas*
- *vice-presidential candidate Gonzalez, Russian delegate Ivanov, agriculture secretary Zaveryukha*
- *shadow cabinet in the United Kingdom*—do not capitalize minister of . . .
- *First Lady Hillary Rodham Clinton*

Avoid preceding a name with more than one title. Use the more important one first, and then the other later in the text—if necessary, or if desired for variation, but make sure the reader understands.

Examples

- *Minister of Defense Yazov . . . Marshal Yazov*
- *President Pinochet . . . General Pinochet*

After or in Place of the Name

Generally, a title standing alone is lowercased unless it refers to the incumbent—present or past (but not future). To indicate preeminence or distinction *in certain instances*, capitalize a common noun title or shortened title when it follows the name of a person or is used alone *in reference to the person to whom the title belongs or belonged.* The plural form of such a title is also capitalized as appropriate. So is the word *Acting* if it is a valid part of a capitalized title. However, do not capitalize such a title when it refers to the office rather than the individual or when it is used generally. Do not capitalize in a personal title the suffixes *-designate* and *-elect*, the prefix *ex-*, or the adjectives *former* and *then* (the exception would be when such a personal title is part of the title of a publication).

Head or assistant head of state or government or a royal heir apparent.

Examples

- *Jacques Chirac, President of France, the President*
- *the Premiers of Italy and France*
- *the Premier-designate, the Vice President–elect*
- *the former Vice President, the ex-President, the ex–Minister of State, the Ambassador-designate*

- *the Queen of England, the Prince of Wales, the Crown Prince*
- *the former King, the then Secretary General, the Under Secretary General*
- *the First Lady, the First Family (*but *the royal family)*

but:

aspire to be president   *the new chief of state*

destined to be king   *ambassador at large*

Specific head or assistant head of a national government unit in the executive branch and principal members of the legislative and judicial branches.

Examples

- *Hedy Fry, the Secretary of State for Multiculturalism and the Status of Women*
- *the Acting Foreign Secretary (*but *the shadow foreign secretary)*
- *the Minister of Foreign Affairs*
- *the Foreign Minister*
- *the Deputy Minister of Foreign Affairs (*but *cabinet ministers and secretaries of state; a deputy minister of foreign affairs, a first deputy premier; shadow minister, shadow chancellor of the Exchequer)*
- *Minister Without Portfolio*
- *the Chief Justice (*but *an associate justice)*
- *the President of the Senate, the President*
- *the Speaker of the House, the Speaker*

but:

- *a senator, a representative*
- *the Member of Parliament (*never parliamentarian*)*
- *the deputy to the National Assembly*
- *chair of the Foreign Affairs Committee*
- *the deputy chair*

Principal officers of party organizations in Communist-ruled countries.

Examples

- *the General Secretary, the party General Secretary*
- *the party secretary responsible for agriculture*
- *a full member or a candidate member of the party Politburo*
- *the general secretary of the Italian Communist Party*

Highest official of a first-order administrative division under a national government or his or her deputy.

Examples

- *the Premier of Quebec, the Vice Premier of Quebec*
- *the Governor of Connecticut*
- *the Lieutenant Governor of Virginia*
- *the Acting Governor of Kentucky*
- *the Republic of Armenia First Secretary*

but:

- *a capable premier*

- *several state governors*
- *the mayor of Philadelphia*

Highest officer in a military service or his deputy.

Examples

- *Commander in Chief of the Chilean Army; the Commander in Chief*
- *Chief of Staff, Brazilian Air Force, Deputy Chief of Staff*
but:
- *the quartermaster*
- *commander, IV Corps*
- *chief, G-2 (Intelligence Branch), Army Headquarters*
- *the general (*military title standing alone is not capitalized*)*

Principal official of an international organization.

Examples

- *the Secretary General*
- *the present Secretaries General of the United Nations and the Organization of American States*
but:
- *periodic selection of NATO secretaries general*

Principal members of the diplomatic corps.

Examples

- *the Ambassador, the British Ambassador*
- *the Minister, the Charge, the Consul General* (but *the consul*)
- *the Deputy Chief of Mission*
but:
- *the defense attache*
- *the counselor of embassy*
- *the economic counselor*
- *the first secretary*
- *the rank of ambassador*
- *ambassadors at the conference* (general use)

Civil or Military

With the exception of *Senator, Representative, Commodore*, and *Commandant*, which are never abbreviated, civil or military titles preceding a name are abbreviated if followed by given name or initial as well as surname. *Doctor* is always abbreviated as a title.

Examples

- *Prof. Mary Jones, Professor Jones; Gen. J. F. Smith* (note space between initials), *General Smith*
- *Representative Henry Brown, Representative Brown*
- *Dr. Robert Young, Dr. Young*

Complimentary

Except in biographic reports, the only title we should use is an official one at the first mention of a person's name. After that, refer to the person by last name or by title, treating males and females alike.

However, in a biographic report mentioning the spouse or other relatives of a person who is the subject of the report, a complimentary title might be needed to ensure clarity.

Examples

- *President Amigo's family will accompany him on the visit. His wife, Dolores, is a concert pianist. Mrs. Amigo, while politically active, has never run for office.*
- *President Amigo's family will accompany her on the visit. Her husband, Luis, is a concert pianist. Mr. Amigo, while politically active, has never run for office.*

Attribution Statements

Titles with names are not necessary in attribution statements. However, there have been rare instances when we have allowed the use of M.D. or Ph.D. after a name.

---

titles of publications

Use italic type for titles of books, periodicals, or works of art (including the performing arts—plays, compositions, broadcasts, films, and so forth). But use quotation marks for titles of articles or other parts within longer works.

Examples

- *a subscription to* The Washingtonian
- *a performance of* The Taming of the Shrew
- *a showing of Leonardo da Vinci's* Mona Lisa
- *appearing on* Inside Washington
- *Henry Smith's 25 April "Controlling Crime" from* The New York Times

Capitalize the first letter of the initial word, that of the final word, and that of any principal word in titles of publications and the like (books, newspapers, magazines, periodicals, articles, series, reports, speeches, plays, movies, and musical compositions, as well as works of art, graphics, tables, chapters and headings, headlines, and historic documents).

Principal words include all nouns, pronouns, verbs (including the *to* in an infinitive), adjectives, and adverbs; the preposition *via*, as well as *per* when part of a unit modifier; all words of more than three letters; the first word following a colon or em dash within a title; and parts of compounds that would be capitalized standing alone.

Examples

Long-Term	*Follow-On*
Re-Creation	*Trade-Off*

but:

Balance-of-Payments Problems   *Co-op Formation*

If a normally lowercased short word is used in juxtaposition with a capitalized word of like significance, it should also be capitalized.

Examples

Buildings In and Near Minneapolis   *Construction "On the Cheap"*

Annotations (such as arrowed captions or callouts) on a photograph, map, or other graphic have only the first letter of the initial word capitalized. If a number given as a figure begins such a caption, the word following it is not capitalized.

Example

• *200-mile limit*

Shortened Titles

The above rule is sometimes modified to apply to accepted shortened titles of some publications and historic documents.

Examples

• *article in* The Washington Post, *quoted in the* Post *article*
• *reported in* The Times, *from the* London Times *(the initial reference to this newspaper should always be worded to avoid confusion with *The New York Times, and vice versa)
• *Quadripartite Agreement, the Agreement*
• *Balfour Declaration, the Declaration (*but *a British white paper)*
but:
• *The 1962 Constitution was a vast improvement over earlier constitutions.*

Foreign Titles

A title in a foreign language may or may not be translated, depending on the title and the context. If a translation is given, it should be in parentheses and in italics. No translation is needed for such familiar titles as *Pravda, Trud, Der Spiegel, Le Monde, Izvestiya, L'Osservatore Romano*, and *Paris Match.*

Some titles have conventionally been cited only in translated form. In such cases, an explanation is more relevant and useful than a translation.

Example

• People's Daily, *official organ of the Chinese Communist Party*

For a foreign-language title, always use the one given on the cover or first page of the publication. This rule does not apply to titles that must be given in a language other than English; capitalization in these titles should conform to the practice in that language.

Laws and Treaties

Capitalize the first word and all important words in the formal titles or distinguishing shortened names of federal, state, or foreign documents. If a descriptive term is used, or if the document is still in draft form, use lowercase. The names of ratified treaties are capitalized when rendered in full. For treaties that have not been ratified, the *t* in treaty should always be lowercase.

Examples

Bill of Rights   *Treaty of Paris, the treaty*   *START Treaty, the treaty*

---

together with

Often found immediately after the subject of a sentence, *together with* phrases do not affect the verb. The same is true of *along with, as well as, in addition to*, and *like*.

Example

- *Lower productivity, together with higher interest rates, is hurting the economy.*

---

too

In the sense of very, *too* is not acceptable in formal writing; in the sense of excessively, however, it is likely to be the best word.

---

toward

Use the American form. We also omit the *s* in all the common words ending in *ward*, such as *afterward, backward, downward, upward, eastward*, and *northward.*

---

trade names

Trade names should be capitalized or, if inappropriate, replaced with a generic term.

Examples

- *air-cushion vehicle (ACV) or hover craft* (unless it is a real Hovercraft)
- *tracked vehicles* (unless they have genuine Caterpillar treads)
- *fiberglass* (unless it is Owens-Corning Fiberglas)
- *a photocopy* (unless it is known to be a Xerox copy or a Kodak copy)
- *a vacuum bottle* (unless it is a real Thermos)

---

traditions

Long-established practices or elements of culture passed down from generation to generation. A *tradition* cannot be established in a few years.

---

transliteration

The Foreign Broadcast Information Service (FBIS) is the authority within the Agency for transliteration systems.

transpire	Had special uses in science, particularly botany, but it is now an acceptable synonym of *happen* or *occur*.
try	Followed by *to*, not and.
type	As a noun, *type* should be followed by *of* in constructions like *that type of plane* or, in the plural, *those types of planes*. The same holds true for *kind* and *sort*. Do not use *type* in apposition with a person or thing. Wording like accommodating-type spokesmen should be shunned.

UK	United Kingdom encompasses Great Britain (England, Scotland, and Wales) and Northern Ireland. *Britain* or *Great Britain* is often used as the shortened form of the country name, but *the United Kingdom* (note the lowercase *t* in *the*) is preferred. *UK* is acceptable as an adjective or, where space is limited and preceded by the definite article, as a noun. *British* is also an acceptable adjective.
UN	United Nations is the preferred noun, and UN is the adjective, except where space is limited.

unit modifiers

The most frequent problem involving compounds is what to do when two or more modifiers immediately precede the word they modify. If the modifiers are coordinate or cumulative—that is, if either could serve as a single modifier—they do not constitute a unit modifier.

Examples

- *migrant construction workers* (not a unit modifier—the modifiers are cumulative because migrant or construction alone could modify workers)
- *40-horsepower engine* (unit modifier—neither 40 nor horsepower could logically serve as a single modifier)
- *carefully prepared report* (unit modifier—only the second word could modify report)

Hyphenated

Unit modifiers immediately preceding the word or words modified are usually hyphenated but sometimes are written as one word.

Examples

1-meter-diameter pipe	*number-one priority*	*US-owned property*
drought-stricken area	*part-time job*	*value-added tax*
English-speaking nation	*still-lingering doubt*	*well-known name*
high-level post	*Third Five-Year Plan*	*yet-undetermined*
low-priced model	*UN-initiated talks*	*outcome*
most-favored-nation clause		
but:		
longtime friend	*policymaking level*	*rightwing group*

Ordinal Numbers

As a general rule retain hyphens in a compound containing an ordinal number used in its literal sense.

Examples

first-quarter report	*second-half performance*
third-country involvement	*eighth-grade class*

but:

first aid station	*Third World delegates*

Prepositional Phrases

Similarly, in a unit modifier containing a prepositional phrase, comprehension is enhanced if hyphens are used for even the best known expressions.

Examples

cost-of-living study	*right-to-work law*
balance-of-payments problem	*under-the-counter sales*

Unhyphenated

When the meaning is clear and readability is not aided, hyphens may be omitted from a compound that precedes the word modified, especially if the compound is an established or familiar phrase. But refrain from an accumulation of modifiers that defies comprehension and impedes readability.

Examples

atomic energy program	*free enterprise system*
ballistic missile early warning radar	*ground attack aircraft*
ballistic missile submarine	*hard currency loan*
civil defense plan	*human rights position*
current account deficit	*natural gas exports*
flight test program	*surface ship deployment*

but:

- *no-hyphen rule* (readability aided); not: no hyphen rule (ambiguous)
- *areas in which ballistic missile submarines normally operate* (readable);
  not: normal ballistic missile submarine operating areas (difficult to comprehend)

In a compound do not hyphenate an adverb ending in *ly.*

Examples

newly elected president	*wholly owned subsidiary*

Conjunctions

No hyphen is required if the compound preceding the word or words modified is already tied together with a conjunction.

Examples

cold but sunny day	*middle or late 1980s*
command and control echelons	*medium and high altitude*

An improvised compound (cliche) such as that in *hard-and-fast rule* or *bread-and-butter issue* is an exception.

Predicates

A unit modifier must be distinguished from a compound predicate adjective, in which the hyphen is usually omitted. In this sense, do not confuse a unit modifier with a hyphenated compound formed by adding a prefix or suffix. Such a compound (for example, *self-educated* and *rent-free*) would retain its hyphen in the predicate form.

Examples

- *His future was still undetermined while he was a student.*
- *Most of the transactions in that deal were foreign financed, and the exchanges were under the counter.*
- *The talks were US initiated, and the agenda well prepared.*
- *The increase was 4 percent in 1990 and 5 percent in 1991.*
- *The majority of the population was English speaking.*
- *The government has been socialist leaning in recent years.*
- *She is self-educated.*

---

units of measure

Metric System

The Intelligence Community usually uses the International System of Units (the metric system).

Use meters or kilometers to express size, specifications, or characteristics of things. Among the excepted units of measure are the kiloton, nautical mile for sea distances, pounds per square inch, and the knot. These units (or Mach units, if appropriate) continue to be used for certain weapon system parameters. Other nonmetric units of measure still in use include barrels (and barrels per day) in reporting on the petroleum industry, the US bushel in reporting on grain production and trade, cubic feet in reporting on natural gas reserves or output, and short tons (not metric tons) in reporting on nuclear weapons (rather than the metric unit joule).

Factors for Converting to Metric Units of Measure

To Convert From	*To*	*Multiply by*
acres	*hectares*	*0.4047*
acres	*square kilometers*	*0.004047*
acres	*square meters*	*4,046.8564*
bushels	*cubic meters*	*0.03524*
degrees Fahrenheit	*degrees Celsius*	*5/9 (after subtracting 32)*
feet	*centimeters*	*30.48*
feet	*meters*	*0.3048*
feet, cubic	*cubic meters*	*0.02832*
feet, square	*square meters*	*0.09290*
gallons, UK (imperial)	*cubic meters*	*0.004546*

gallons, UK (imperial)	liters	4.5461
gallons, US	cubic meters	0.003785
gallons, US	liters	3.7854
inches	centimeters	2.54
inches	meters	0.0254
inches, cubic	cubic meters	0.00001639
inches, square	square centimeters	6.4516
inches, square	square meters	0.0006452
miles, nautical	kilometers	1.852
miles, nautical	meters	1,852
miles, nautical, square	square kilometers	3.4299
miles, statute	meters	1,609.344
miles, statute	kilometers	1.6093
miles, statute, square	hectares	258.9988
miles, statute, square	square kilometers	2.5900
ounces, avoirdupois	grams	28.3495
ounces, troy	grams	31.1035
pints, liquid	liters	0.4732
pounds, avoirdupois	kilograms	0.4536
pounds, troy	grams	373.2417
pounds per square inch	kilopascals	6.8948
quarts, liquid	liters	0.9464
tons, long	metric tons	1.0160
tons, short	metric tons	0.9072
yards	meter	0.9144
yards, cubic	cubic meters	0.7646
yards, square	square meters	0.8361

Figures With Units of Measure

Figures (not words) are used with any unit of measure (excluding units of time).

Examples

- *The project involved the use of pipe 48 inches (about 120 centimeters) in diameter.*
- *Each slab weighed nearly 50 kilograms.*
- *They advanced several hundred kilometers (never several hundred km).*
- *A temperature below 5 degrees Celsius (or 5°C) would impede operation of the system.*
- *Each mobile was suspended by a 2-meter (never 2-m) wire. (Avoid numerical unit modifiers with single-letter symbols; spell out, or change to 200-cm.)*

Scale

If elements in a scale represent equal units of measure, the scale is expressed as a ratio.

Example

- *1:45 or 1 part represents 45 parts*

However, if two different units of measure are involved, the style is as follows.

Example

- *1 nm = 1.852 km* or *1 nautical mile equals 1.852 kilometers*

Symbols

The National Bureau of Standards holds that shortened forms used to represent units of measure should be called symbols, rather than abbreviations, because no periods are used. Do not add an "s" after the symbol to make it plural. Do not abbreviate a unit of measure used in a general or approximate (dataless) sense. Do not abbreviate or use symbols for one or just a few isolated units of measure within text even when precise quantities are given. But do abbreviate units of measure used frequently or fairly frequently throughout the text of a report. Avoid numerical unit modifiers with single-letter symbols (see page 118).

Standard Symbols for Units of Measure

A	*ampere, angstrom*	*dL*	*deciliter*
ac	*alternating current*	*dm*	*decimeter*
AF	*audiofrequency*	*dwt*	*deadweight ton*
Ah	*ampere-hour*	*EHF*	*extremely high frequency*
A/m	*ampere per meter*	*emu*	*electromagnetic unit*
AM	*amplitude modulation*	*F*	*Fahrenheit (degree), farad*
avdp	*avoirdupois*	*FM*	*frequency modulation*
b	*bit*	*ft*	*foot*
b/d	*barrels per day*	*G*	*giga (prefix, 1 billion)*
Btu	*British thermal unit*	*g*	*gram, acceleration of gravity*
bu	*bushel*	*gal/min*	*gallons per minute*
C	*Celsius (degrees)*	*gal/s*	*gallons per second*
c	*cycle (radio)*	*GHz*	*gigahertz*
cL	*centiliter*		*(gigacycles per second)*
cm	*centimeter*	*h*	*hour*
c/m	*cycles per minute*	*ha*	*hectare*
cu	*cubic*	*HF*	*high frequency*
cwt	*hundredweight*	*hg*	*hectogram*
da	*deka*	*hL*	*hectoliter*
dag	*dekagram*	*hm*	*hectometer*
daL	*dekaliter*	*hp*	*horsepower*
dam	*dekameter*	*hph*	*horsepower-hour*
dB	*decibel*	*Hz*	*hertz (cycles per second)*
dBu	*decibel unit*	*in*	*inch*
dBsm	*decibels relative to*	*J*	*joule*
	1 square meter	*J/K*	*joule per kelvin*
dc	*direct current*	*K*	*kelvin (degree not used)*
dg	*decigram*	*k*	*kilo, thousand*
			(7k = 7,000)

KB	*kilobyte*	*mm*	*millimeter*
kc	*kilocycle*	*MMt*	*million metric tons*
kg	*kilogram*	*mph*	*miles per hour*
kHz	*kilohertz (kilocycles per second)*	*Mt*	*megaton*
		mV	*millivolt*
kL	*kiloliter*	*MW*	*megawatt*
km	*kilometer*	*mW*	*milliwatt*
km²	*square kilometers*	*n*	*nano (prefix, one-billionth)*
km/h	*kilometer per hour*	*nA*	*nanoampere*
kn	*knot (speed)*	*nm*	*nautical mile*
kt	*kiloton*	*ns*	*nanosecond*
kV	*kilovolt*	*oz*	*ounce (avoirdupois)*
kVA	*kilovoltampere*	*p*	*pico (prefix, one-trillionth)*
kW	*kilowatt*	*pA*	*picoampere*
kWh	*kilowatthour*	*pH*	*hydrogen-ion concentration*
L	*liter*	*ps*	*picosecond*
lb	*pound*	*psi*	*pounds per square inch*
LF	*low frequency*	*pt*	*pint*
L/s	*liters per second*	*pW*	*picowatt*
M	*million (3M = 3 million)*	*qt*	*quart*
m	*meter*	*quad*	*quadrillion*
m³	*cubic meters*	*rad*	*radian*
μ	*micro (prefix, one-millionth)*	*rms*	*root mean square*
μF	*microfarad*	*rpm*	*revolutions per minute*
mA	*milliampere*	*rps*	*revolutions per second*
mbar	*millibar*	*s*	*second*
mb/d	*million barrels per day*	*T*	*tera (prefix, 1 trillion)*
Mc	*megacycle*	*ton*	*US ton (not abbreviated)*
mc	*millicycle*	*UHF*	*ultrahigh frequency*
mg	*milligram*	*V*	*volt*
MHz	*megahertz*	*VA*	*voltampere*
mHz	*millihertz*	*VHF*	*very high frequency*
min	*minute*	*V/m*	*volt per meter*
MJ	*megajoule*	*W*	*watt*
mL	*milliliter*	*Wh*	*watthour*

upbeat, downbeat

Use only as musical terms.

upcoming, forthcoming, coming

Instead of using *upcoming*, when you are looking for an adjective meaning to take place later, try *forthcoming* or just *coming*. Or give a clue as to when: next week, next month.

upon, on, up on	In almost all cases you can substitute *on* for *upon* as a preposition (*bearing on the case*). Do not change *upon* as an adverb (*he felt overworked and put upon*). *Up on* can be an adverb and preposition (*living up on the third floor*).
US	*US*, not American, is the preferred adjective for our country. *United States* (written out) is the preferred noun, but *the US* may be used when repetition or space is a problem. Try also using *Washington* as the noun when it is clear that you are referring to the US Government, not the capital city. U.S. is used on maps.
usage	Does not equate to use. *Usage* means either a manner of use, as in *rough usage*, or a habitual practice creating a standard, as in *good English usage*.

variety of	A phrase that sometimes conveys the plural sense of *several* or *various* is *variety of*.

Example

• *A variety of sources report high casualties.*

But when the emphasis is on the singular *variety*, rather than on the plural object of *of*, the verb is singular.

Example

• *A variety of meals is better than eating the same food all the time.*

verbal, oral	*Verbal* and *oral* are not synonyms. A *verbal* message can be either spoken or written. An *oral* message is always spoken.
very, definitely	Use *very, definitely*, and other ambiguous intensifiers sparingly.
via, per	Though only prepositions, with fewer than four letters, *via* and *per* are capitalized in titles.
viable	Denotes the capacity of a newly created organism to maintain a separate existence. It is often mistakenly used when *durable, lasting, workable, effective*, or *practical* is the appropriate adjective.

we, us, our, ours	Should never be used when referring to the United States. The first person plural is reserved in intelligence writing for the analysts/estimators/writers themselves.
weather	Capitalize *hurricane* as part of a US National Weather Service name for such a storm, as in *Hurricane Gilbert*. The term changes to *typhoon* over the Pacific Ocean and, again, is capitalized when part of a personalized name, such as *Typhoon Ruby*. Both terms designate types of *cyclones*, as does *tornado*, but *cyclones* and *tornadoes* remain lowercase, as does a *waterspout* (a tornado gone to sea).
whether or not	*Whether* does not always need *or not*.

whether or not

Examples

- *He still has not decided whether to go.*
- *She is going whether or not he does.*

which

Introduces a nonrestrictive clause—a phrase that is unessential but adds information. A nonrestrictive clause is preceded and followed by commas.

while

As a conjunction, *while* usually has reference to time.

Example

- *While the President was out of the country, the Army staged a coup.*

It can, with discretion, also be used in the sense of *although* or of *but*.

Example

- *While he hated force, he recognized the need for order.*

Avoid using *while* in the sense of "and."

who, whom

Who (nominative case) and *whom* (objective case) are usually not that difficult to grasp.

Examples

- *Who is his boss?*
- *Whom does she work for?*

But occasionally it is difficult, as when the syntax makes *who* or *whoever* sound more objective than nominative.

Examples

- *The voters will pick the candidate who they think will do the best job.*
- *The voters will turn against whoever they think is responsible for their economic hardships. (*Whomever seems to be the object of the preposition, but the object of *against* is not a single word but the whole clause *whoever . . . is responsible for their economic hardships.)*

---

whose | Functions as the possessive of both *who* and *which*.

---

wide | Any capitalized word ending in the suffix *wide* is spelled with a hyphen (*Agency-wide*). Most uncapitalized words ending with the suffix *wide* are one word (*nationwide*).

---

widows/orphans | A *widow line* is a single line at the top of a page—usually the last line of a paragraph. An *orphan line* is a single line at the bottom of a page—usually the first line of a paragraph. Avoid both.

---

with | *With* does not have the conjunctive role of "and."

Examples

- *They are married and have children. (*Not: They are married, with children.*)*
- *He is married and has a child. (*Not: He is married with one child.*)*

Too often *with* is used to attach an additional thought to a sentence that would be better treated as an independent clause following an *and* or a *semicolon.*

Example

- *Economics and history are his mainstays; knowledge of linguistics is an additional qualification. (*Not: Economics and history are his mainstays, with knowledge of linguistics an additional qualification.*)*

---

word breaks | Do not break the last word in a paragraph, with only a partial word for the line.

Break words ending in a slash (/) after the slash, with no hyphen.

Do not break most abbreviations or acronyms. However, in the case of a very long abbreviation or acronym, break it, without a hyphen, after letters denoting a complete word.

Example

- *CINC SOUTHCOM*

Homographs

Words with the same spelling but different meaning and often with different pronunciation may be divided differently. One group of homographs is divided on the base word when *er* is added to indicate a person or device performing the action of the base word.

Examples

- *coun-ter (against); count-er (one who counts)*
- *foun-der (to sink); found-er (one who originates)*

Another group is divided differently according to pronunciation.

Examples

- *at-tri-bute (n); at-trib-ute (v)*
- *de-sert (something deserved, to abandon); des-ert (barren land)*
- *in-va-lid (not well); in-val-id (not valid)*

youth

As the opposite of old age, *youth* is always singular. When it means young persons (male or female) collectively, it is always plural. When the word refers to an individual young male it is, of course, singular, and its plural is *youths*.

Examples

- *The nation's youth were encouraged to enroll.*
- *A gang of youths started the riot.*

zero

Supply a zero before a decimal point when there is no whole unit, except in the case of weapons calibers or ammunition.

Examples

0.24 centimeter   *silver 0.900 fine*

but:

.30 caliber

Retain zeros after a decimal point only for exact measurements or to maintain parallelism in a series of numbers or in tabular material.

Compound Words/Spelling

aberration

able-bodied (um)

ABM (antiballistic missile) system

about-face

above-average (um)

aboveboard

above-cited

abovedeck

aboveground (um)

above ground (pred)

above-mentioned

above-named

above water (pred)

above-water (um)

abridgment

absentminded

Abu Nidal organization

accede

access code (comp)

accessible

access time (comp)

accommodate

accords (Geneva, Helsinki, Amman, Camp David, Dayton, Paris)

accoutrement

Achilles' heel

acknowledgment

ACL (comp, access control list)

acoustic coupler (comp)

acquiesce (takes the preposition *in*, not to)

across-the-board (um)

active-duty (um)

A.D. (*anno domini*, precedes number)

adapter (comp)

addendum, addenda (pl)

additionally (adv of addition; do not use for in addition)

add-on (n)

ad hoc

adjutants general

ad lib (adv)

ad-lib (adj, n, v), ad-libbed, ad-libbing

admissible

advertise

advise

adviser

advisory

aegis

affect (v, influence)

Afghan army

afore (cf, all one word)

A-frame

Africaans (language)

Africa-wide

after (cf, all one word)

afterglow

afterward

agenda(s)

agents-of-influence (um)

age-old

aging

agitprop

agree (*with* a person, *to* a proposal, *on* a plan)

agreed-to (um)

agreed-upon (um)

agro (cf, all one word)

agroindustrial

aid (n, assistance; v, assist)

aide (assistant)

aide(s)-de-camp

aide-memoire (memory jog), aides-memoires (pl)

AIDS (acquired immuno-deficiency syndrome)

aim point

air and sea ports

airbag

airbase

air-based (um)

airblast

airborne warning and control system (AWACS) aircraft

air-breathing

airburst

aircargo

air-condition, air-conditioner, air-conditioning

air cover

aircraft

air crash

aircrew

air-cushion vehicle (ACV)

air defense (n, um)

air-dried (um)

airdrop (n, v)

airdroppable

airfield

air fleet

airflow

airframe

air-handling (um)

airhead

air intercept (n, um)

airlanded, airlanding

air-launched (um)

airlift

airline

airlink

airmail

airman

airmass

airmobile

airpower (*but* naval and air power)

air quality (um)

air raid

air show

airspace

airspeed

airstrike (*but* naval and air strike)

airstrip

airtight

air time (broadcast media)

air vent

air war

airwave

airway

airworthy

a.k.a. (also known as)

alias(es)

align, aligned, alignment

all-absorbing (um)

all-around (um)

all-clear (n, um)

all-day

Alliance, Allied, Allies (in reference to NATO, otherwise lowercase)

all-inclusive (um)

all-knowing

allophone

all-out

all ready (prepared)

all right

all-round (um)

all-source (adj)

all-star

alltime (adj)

all time (n, full time)

all together (collectively, in unison)

all-weather

alongside

a lot

allot, allotted, allotting

AlphaJet

alphanumeric (comp)

already (previous)

also-ran(s)

alternate (rotating, following by turns)

alternative (pertains to a choice between possibilities)

altogether (completely)

a.m.

aluminum

alumna, alumnae (feminine)

alumnus, alumni (masculine)

ambassador(s) at large

Ambassador-designate (see p.108)

ambi (cf, all one word)

    ambidextrous

American-flag ship

amidships

amino (as prefix, all one word)

amino acid

Amman accords

among (use when the relationship of more than two things is vague or collective)

amorphous

An-12 Cub

analog (comp), **analogue** (all other meanings)

analysis

analytic (adj)

analyze

anchorperson

and/or (use sparingly)

anemia

anesthetic

aneurysm

anglophone (um)

Anglophone (n)

annul, annulled, annulling, annulment

anomalous

anonymous

antedate

antenna(s)

antennae (pl, zoology)

anti (pref, usually one word)

antiaircraft

anti-American

antiapartheid

anti-arms-control

antiballistic missile (n, um, **ABM**)

antibiotic (adj)

antibiotic(s) (n)

antichrist

anti-cruise-missile

antidefense

antiestablishment

anti-guided-missile (um)

antigunrunning

anti-imperial

anti-inflation, anti-inflationary

anti-insurgent

antimissile

anti-money-laundering (um)

anti-nuclear-weapons

antiradiation

antiradiation-homing (adj)

anti-Semitism

antiship-cruise-missile (um)

anti-ship cruise missile

anti-submarine-warfare (um)

anti-tactical-ballistic missile (**ATBM**)

anti-tactical-ballistic-missile (um)

antitank guided missile

antivirus program (comp)

antiwar

antipathy

anybody

anyone

any time

anyway (adv)

APEC (Asia Pacific Economic Cooperation)

API (comp, application program interface)

apocalypse

appall, appalled, appalling

apparatus(es)

appealing

appendix B

appendix(es)

applet (comp)

apprehensible

April Fools' Day

a priori

A-priority

Arab-Israeli war

Aramco

Archie (comp)

arched-roof (adj)

archenemy

archeology

archrival

arch roofed (um)

archtype, archetypical

arise

armor-heavy (um)

arms control

arms-exporting

arm's-length (adj)

arm's length (n)

armsmaker

arms-producing

arms-supplying

arm-twisting (n)

army-group-level (um)

armywide, Army-wide

around-the-clock (um)

artificial intelligence (comp)

artificial language (comp)

artilleryman

artspeak

artwork

ascendancy, ascendant

ascent (rise)

ASCII (comp, American Standard Code for Information Interchange)

Asia Pacific Economic Cooperation (*but* Asia-Pacific region)

assassinate

assembly line

assemblyman

assent (consent)

assistant comptrollers general

asylee (designates a person seeking asylum or one given asylum)

Atlantic-to-the-Urals zone

ATBM (anti-tactical-ballistic missile)

at-large (um)

atomic energy (n, um)

at-sea (um)

attache(s)

attorneys general

audible

audiocassette

audiosurveillance

audiotape

audiovisual

augur (v, to predict from signs or omens)

authoring (comp)

authority (comp)

automaker

autoworker

auxiliary

AWACS (airborne warning and control system)

avant-garde

awhile (adv, for a time)

a while (n, a period of time)

axis, axes (pl)

B.A. (bachelor of arts)

baby boomer

bachelor's degree (B.A.)

backbencher

backbite (v)

back bonding

backbone (comp)

back burner

back channel (n)

back-channel (v, um)

back door (n)

backdoor (um)

back down (v)

backdown (n)

backfit

background processing (comp)

backlash

backpay

backpedal (v)

backroad

backroom

backseat

backslide

backstage

backstopped

backtrack

backup (n, um)

back up (v)

backup system (comp)

backward (no "s")

backwater

backyard

bagful

bag lady

Bahamas (The) (n)

bailout (n, um)

bail out (v)

balance-of-payments (adj)

Balkanize

ball bearing

ballistic missile (um, of submarines defense, radar)

ballistic missile early warning (BMEW) radar

ballistic-missile-related (um)

ballistic missile submarine (SSB)

ballpark

Baltic republics/states (not the Baltics)

bandwagon

bandwidth (radar)

banknote

bankrupt, bankrupted, bankrupting

Barclays Bank

bar code (comp)

barebones (nonliteral)

base camp

baseline

basis, bases (pl)

bathroom

battalion

battlefront

battleground

battle group

battleline

battle management (n, um)

battle readiness

battle-ready (um)

BBS (comp, bulletin board system)

B.C. (before Christ, comes after the number)

beam width

Bear G('s)

bedouin (sing, pl)

bed rest

bed rock

beekeeper

behind-the-scenes (adj)

belowground

below-market (um)

belt-tightening

beltway bandit

benchmark (nonliteral)

beneficient

benefit, benefited, benefiting

Benelux

Berlin Wall (the Wall)

beside (alongside)

besides (except, other than)

best seller

bete noire, betes noires (pl)

better-than-even (um)

beyond-visual-range (BVR) air-to-air missile

BGN (Board on Geographic Names, the authority for place name spellings)

bi (pref)

> bi-iliac
> *rest one word*

biannually (twice a year)

bias, biased, biases, biasing

biennially (once every two years)

Big Four

big-power (adj)

big shot

big-ticket (adj)

binary system (comp)

BIOS (comp, basic input/output system)

bird's-eye (adj)

birdshot

birdwatching

birthplace

birthrate

bistatic

bit map (n)

bit-map (v)

bit-mapped (um)

bit mapping (comp)

biweekly (once every two weeks)

blacklist

black market (n)

black-market (um, v)

black-marketeer

blastmark

blastproof

blessed

blind eye

blitzkrieg(s)

bloc (group)

block (form)

block command (comp)

blond

bloodbath

bloodletting

blood pressure

bloodthirsty

blowdown

blowout (n, adj)

blow out (v)

blue-chip (adj)

blue chip (n)

blue-collar (nonliteral adj)

blue-pencil (v, adj)

blueprint

blue-ribbon (nonliteral adj)

blue-water navy

boardroom

boatbuilding

boathouse

boatload

boat people

boatyard

body bag

bodyguard

body politic

Boeing 747(s)

boiler plate

boldface

bomb bay

bombdrop

bomb load

bombmaker, bombmaking

bombproof

bombsight

bombsquad

bona fide (adj)

bona fides (n, sing and pl)

boobytrap, boobytrapped, boobytrapping

bookkeeping

bookmark (comp)

bookseller

bookstore

Boolean logic (comp)

boot camp

bootleg software (comp)

border guard (n, um)

borderland

borderline

boresight

border post

born (given birth)

born-again (n, adj)

borne (carried)

bottleneck

bottom-line (adj)

bourgeoisie (n, middle class)

boxcar

boxlike

bps (comp, bits per second)

brain child

brain trust

brainwash

brand name (um)

breach (gap)

bread-and-butter (adj)

breadbasket

breakdown (n, um)

break down (v)

break even (v)

break-even (um)

break-in (n, adj)

break in (v)

breakout (n, um)

break out (v)

breakpoint

breakthrough

breakup (n, um)

break up (v)

breathtaking

breech (lower part)

breeding ground

bridgebuilder

bridgehead

bridgeway

bridgework

briefcase

brinkmanship

broadband (um)

broad-based

broadburst

broadcast

broadcloth

broad gauge (n)

broad-gauge (adj)

broadleg (n, adj)

broadminded

broad-scoped (um)

broken-down (um)

brother(s)-in-law

brunet

brushpass

bucketful

budget-busting (um)

building block (n)

building-block (adj)

buildup (n, adj)

build up (v)

built-in (um)

built-up (um)

bulletin board

bulletproof

bullheaded

burdensharing

bureau(s)

burgeoning (describes something that is newly emerging, not simply growing)

burn bag

burned

burnout (n)

burnup

bus, bused, buses, busing

busdriver

busfare

businesslike

busline

busload

busting (use in terms like budget busting and trust busting)

buy-back (um)

buy in (v)

buyout (n, adj)

buy out (v)

buzzword

BW-agent (um)

by (cf, usually one word)

    byelection

    bylaw

    bypass

    byproduct

cache (comp)

CAD/CAM (comp, computer-aided design/computer-aided manufacturing)

CADD (comp, computer-aided design and drafting)

CAL (comp, computer-augmented learning)

caldron

caliber (.22-caliber pistol)

call back (v)

callback (n, adj)

call-in (adj)

call in (v)

callous (adj)

call sign

call up (v)

callup (n, um)

callus (n)

camouflage

cancel, canceled, cancelable, canceling (*but* **cancellation**)

candor

canister

cannon, cannons (pl when referred to individually) or **cannon** (pl when referred to collectively)

cannot

canoeing

canvas (cloth)

canvas-covered (um)

canvass (solicit)

capital (city, money)

capital-intensive (um)

capitol (building)

carat (weight)

carbarn

car bomb, car bomb, car-bombing, car-bombed (n)

car-bomb (adj)

car-bomb(ing) (v)

carbon monoxide

carcinogen(ic)

card-carrying (adj)

carefree

caret (insertion mark)

car ferry

Caribbean basin

carline

carload

car-mile

carpal tunnel syndrome

carrier-based (um)

carrierborne

carry over (v)

carryover (n, adj)

carte blanche, cartes blanches (pl)

cartel (even with specific name)

Cartesian coordinates (comp)

cartilage

car wash

case-by-case (adj)

caseload

case officer (C/O)

caseworker

cash-and-carry (adj)

cash-flow (n, adj)

cashier's check

cash-strapped (um)

cast off (v)

castoff (n, um)

casual (unimportant)

casualties (include persons injured, captured, or missing in action as well as those killed in battle)

casus belli (sing and pl)

catalog, cataloged, cataloging, cataloger

cat-and-mouse (um)

catchall (n, um)

catchphrase

catch up (v)

catch-up (n, adj)

catchword

cat's-paw

catsup

cattle breeder

cattleman

cattle raiser

cattle-raising (um)

cattle ranch

catwalk

caudillo(s)

causal (of cause)

cause celebre, causes celebres (pl)

causeway

cave in (v)

cave-in (n, um)

CD ROM (comp, compact disk read-only memory)

cease fire (v)

cease-fire (n, um)

Celsius

cementmaking

census taker

census-taking (um)

center (as a verb, is used with *on*, *upon*, *in*, or *at*, but not around)

center-left

centerline

centerpiece

centerpole

center-right

centi (cf, all one word)

centri (cf, all one word)

CERN (European Organization for Nuclear Research)

CFE Treaty

CGA (comp, Color Graphics Adapter)

CGI (comp, Common Gateway Interface)

chain of command

chainsmoke (v)

chainsmoker (n)

chairperson

chancellery

chancellor

chancellor-candidate

chancery

changeable

change over (v)

changeover (n, adj)

channel, channeled, channeling

chaperon

chapter 3

charge-coupled

charge(s) d'affaires

chartroom

chassis (sing and pl)

chastise

chateau(s)

chauvinism

checkbook (n)

check-clearing

check in (v)

check-in (n, adj)

checklist

check out (v)

checkout (n, adj)

checkpoint

checksheet

check up (v)

checkup (n, adj)

check valve

checkwriting

chef de cabinet

chemical-weapons-free (um)

chemical-weapons-related (um)

cherrypicker

chiefs of staff

child care

childlike

chisel, chiseled, chiseler, chiseling

chitchat

chlorofluorocarbons

chokepoint

Chunnel (Eurotunnel)

church (the, *but* Catholic Church)

churchgoer, churchgoing

CI (um, counterintelligence)

CIALink (comp)

c.i.f. (cost, insurance, and freight)

cigarette

circa

circuit breaker

citable

City, The (London financial district)

city dweller

citywide

civil defense (n, um)

clamor

clamp down (v)

clampdown (n)

clean room

clean up (v)

cleanup (n, um)

clear-cut (distinct)

clearcut (n, v, forestry)

clearheaded

clearinghouse

clear up (v)

clearup (n)

cleave, clove, cloven

clew up (nautical)

cliche(s)

climactic (climax, highest point)

climatic (of climate, weather)

clip art (comp)

clockwise

closed-circuit (adj)

closed-door (adj)

close-in (um)

close-knit

closemouthed

close out (v)

closeout (n, adj)

close-range (um)

close up (v)

closeup (n, um)

cloth-backed (um)

clothbound

clothesline

C/O (case officer)

co (pref)

co-deputy-chair

co-op, co-opt, co-optation

co-owner

co-vice-chair

rest one word

coauthor

cochair

coexist

cofounder

cooperate

coorbital

coprocessor (comp)

coproduction

co-worker

coalbed

coal-black (um)

coalboat

coal car

coalfield

coal gas

coal-laden (um)

coal mine(r)

coal-mining (um)

coalpit

coal-slurry (um)

coast guard
but US Coast Guard

coastline

COBOL (comp, common business-oriented language)

coca grower(s), coca growing

cocaine

COCOM (Coordinating Committee on Export Controls)

COCOM-controlled (um)

coconut

c.o.d. (cash on delivery)

coding-off

codename

codeword

coffeegrower, coffeegrowing

coffeehouse

coke oven

coldblooded, coldbloodedness

cold boot (comp)

cold-roll, cold-rolled (v)

cold shoulder (n)

cold-shoulder (v)

Cold War

collapsible

collateral

collocate

colloquy

colossal

combat, combatant, combated, combating

combat-capable (um)

combat-ready (um)

combat support (n, adj)

combined-arms (adj)

combustible

comeback (n)

comedown (n)

come-on (n)

comeuppance

command and control

command, control, and communications (C3)

command, control, communications, computers, and intelligence (C4I)

command driven (comp)

commander(s) in chief

commando(s)

command post

commingle

commiserate

commit, committed, committing

common law

commonplace

common sense (n)

commonsensible

commonwealth

communication buffer (comp)

communications system

communique(s)

Community-wide (Intelligence Community)

communitywide

companywide

compatible

compel, compelled, compelling (to drive or urge forcefully)

compendium(s)

complement (complete)

compliment (praise)

compose (to constitute or to make up)

comprehensible

comprise (to contain or to consist of)

compromise

computer-aided design (um, CAD)

computer-generated (um)

comsat (communications satellite)

concede

concerted (meaning combined, requires a plural subject or object)

conclave (secret meeting, not just any gathering)

concomitant

condominium(s)

cone-shaped (um)

confectionery

confidant (n)

confidence- and security-building (um)

confidence-building (um)

confident (adj)

confrotalk

congressional (non-US)

Congressional (US)

connect time (comp)

connoisseur

consensus (an opinion held collectively, not simply by a majority)

consortium(s)

Constitution (a country's)

constitution (a state's)

consul (n, officer in foreign service)

consuls general

consumer price index

consummate

containership

contemptible

continental shelf

contra (pref)

contra-acting

contra-approach

contra-ion

rest one word

contraband (no "s")

Contras

control, controllable, controlled, controlling

CONUS

converter (comp)

convertible

conveyor

coolheaded

coolly

Copper Belt (Zaire, Zambia)

copper mine(r)

copperplate

copper-plated (um)

copperworker

copperworks

cornerstone

corngrowing

cornmeal

corollary

corona wire (comp)

corps (sing and pl)

corral, corralled, corralling

corroborate

cost-cutting (n, um)

cost-effective (adj)

cost-effectiveness (n)

cost-free (adj)

cost-of-living (um)

cost-reduction (um)

couch potato

council (n, deliberative assembly, its works or membership)

councilor (council member)

counsel (n, v, advice and the person offering it), **counseled, counseling**

counselor (adviser)

counter (cf)

counter-countermeasures

rest one word

counterclockwise

counterintelligence (C/I)

counterrevolutionaries

counterstealth

country-specific (um)

country-western

countrywide

coupmaker

courthouse

court-martial (v, n, singular)

courts-martial (n, plural)

court-martialed (participle)

covername

coversheet

cover story

cover up (v)

coverup (n, um)

cps (comp, characters per second)

CPU (comp, central processing unit)

crack (cocaine)

crack down (v)

crackdown (n, um)

crackhead

cradle-to-grave (um)

crankcase

crank-driven (um)

crankshaft

crash-land (v)

crash landing (n)

credence (belief or mental acceptance)

credible (worthy of belief and judged plausible)

credibility (the quality of being believable)

credit card (um)

credit-starved (um)

creditworthiness

crewmember

crew-training (um)

crimewave

crisis; crises (pl)

crisscross

criterion (sing rarely used), **criteria**

crop-dusting (n)

crop index

crop-year

cross-border

crossbreed

cross-channel

cross-check

cross-connect

cross-country (adj)

crosscurrent

crosscut, crosscutting

cross-examination

cross-examine

crossfire

cross-functional

crosshaul

crossline (n, um)

cross-national (adj)

crossover (n)

cross-pressure

cross-purposes

crossrange

cross-reference

crossroads

cross section

cross-strait (um)

cross-target

crosstrading

crosstrained

crosswalk

crosswise

cruise missile (n, um)

cruise-missile-armed (um)

cruise-missile-related (um)

cryptanalysis

crypto (cf)

crypto-Christian

rest one word

crystal-clear (um)

crystalline

crystallize

culminate (takes the preposition *in*)

Cultural Revolution

cum laude

cure-all (n)

current account (n, um)

current-generation (um)

curriculum(s)

cursor (comp)

custom-built (um)

custom-made (um)

cutaway

cutback (n)

cut in (v)

cut-in (n)

cut off (v)

cutoff (n, um)

cutouts (n)

cutover (adj, of timberland)

cutrate (adj)

cutting-edge (um)

cutthroat

cybernation

cyberspace (comp)

czar

dairy farm

dairyman

damsite

dancercize

darkhorse (nonliteral)

database

data link (comp)

data print

data-processing (um)

data transfer rate (comp)

dateline

date stamp

datum (sing rarely used), data

daughter(s)-in-law

day-care (um)

day-in, day-out (um)

daylong

day school

day shift

daytime

day-to-day

dayworker

D-day

D-day plus 4

de (pref, all one word)

    deenergize

    deice

deaddrop (nonliteral)

dead end

dead heat

dead-in-the-water (um)

deadline

deadload

deadlock

deadpan

deadweight (n, um)

deadwood

dealmaker

dealmaking

deathbed

deathblow

deathlike

death rate

death squad

debris

debt-rescheduling (um)

debt service

decadelong, decades-long (pl)

decadent

decade-old

decisionmaker

decisionmaking
    but
    economic decision making (spell as two words when adj modifies only decision)

deckhand

deductible

deemphasize

deep cover

deep-ocean (um)

deep-sea (adj)

deep-seated (um)

deep-space (adj)

deep underground

deepwater (um)

de-escalte

de facto

defense

defense attache

defense-industrial (um)

defensible

defuse (to remove fuse)

degrees Celsius (Fahrenheit)

deja vu

de jure

delimiter (comp)

delink

Delta-II(s)

demagogue

demarcation

demarche(s)

denial

denouement(s)

deorbit

dependent (n, adj)

deploy (applies only to military movement)

deprecate (express disapproval of something)

depreciate (besides its applications to prices and values, means to belittle something)

depth charge

deputy chief(s) of staff

Deputy Permanent Representative to the United Nations

descendant (n, adj)

desiccate

desktop (comp)

desperate (despondent)

despise

detente

deter, deterred, deterrence, deterrent, deterring

detriment

deutsche mark

devastate

develop, developed, developing, development

developed-country (adj)

developing-country (adj)

device (n)

devise (v)

devotee(s)

dexterous

di (pref, all one word)

diagram, diagramed, diagraming (*but* diagrammatic)

dialogue

diehard (um)

diesel-driven (um)

diesel-electric

diesel engine

diffuse (to spread)

DIP (comp, dual in-line package)

directed-energy (adj)

direction-finding (um)

director(s) general

disaster, disastrous

discernible

discreet (cautious, prudent)

discrete (separate, distinct)

discussible

disequilibrium(s)

disguise

disinformation (the deliberate planting of false reports)

disinterested (impartial)

disk

disparate (different)

dispatch

dispel, dispelled, dispelling

dispersible

dissension

distill, distilled, distilling, distillation

distributor

districtwide

dithered image (comp)

divisible

dockworker

doctrinaire

DoD (Department of Defense)

dogfight

doggerel

dogma(s)

dollar-peso exchange rate

donor-country (um)

doomsday

Doppler

DOS (comp, disk operating system)

dossier

double-agent (adj)

double-barrel (adj)

double-barreled (um)

double-check (v)

double check (n)

double-count (um, v)

double cross (n)

double-cross (v)

double-crosser

doubledeal, doubledealing (v)

double-decker

double-digit (adj)

double-duty (adj)

double-edged (um)

double-entry (um)

double play

double space

doubletalk

double time

double-track (adj, v)

down-and-out (um)

dovetail (v)

downcast

downdraft

downfall

downflow

downgrade

downhill

downline

down-link

download (comp)

downpayment

downplay

downpour

downrange

downriver

downside

downsize

downstream

downswing

downtime

down-to-earth

downtrend

downturn

downward

downwind

draconian measures

draft

draft age (um)

DRAM (comp, dynamic random-access memory)

drawbridge

drawdown (n, um)

drawn-out (um)

drive-by (um)

drive-in (n, adj)

drive shaft

drive-through (adj)

drive up (v)

drive-up (adj)

drop off (v)

dropoff (n, adj)

drop out (v)

dropout (n, adj)

drop text

drought

droughtlike

drought-stricken (um)

drug czar

drug-free (um)

drug lord

drug money (n, um)

drug-producing (um)

drug-smuggling (um)

drug-trafficking (um)

dry cleaner (n, um)

drycleaning

drydock

dry-season (adj)

dual-purpose (adj)

dual-use (adj)

due date

dues-paying (um)

dumpsite

duo (cf, all one word)

dutybound

duty-free (um, adv)

dyeing (coloring)

dying (near death)

Dylux

dynamos

dysfunction, dysfunctional

18-year-olds

earful

early-1980s-vintage (adj)

early or mid-1990s

early or mid-March

early-model (adj)

early-to-mid(dle) 1990s

early-to-mid-March

early warning (um, of radar)

earthmover

earthmoving

east-southeast

eastward

easygoing

Economic and Monetary Union (EMU), a.k.a. European monetary union

economic decision making

economic policy making

Ecuadorian

edgewise

edible

editor(s) in chief

EDP (comp, electronic data processing)

effect (n, result, outcome; v, bring about, perform)

EGA (comp, Enhanced Graphics Adapter)

ego(s)

either (as a subject, takes a singular verb and pronoun)

elan

elbowroom

eldercare

elect (suffix, hyphenated)

President-elect

Senator-elect

election (singular unless the context is plainly plural, as in the last four national elections)

electro (cf)

electro-optics

electro-ultrafiltration

rest one word

electromagnetic

electrotechnics

eleventh-hour (adj)

elicit (to draw out), elicited, eliciting

eligible

elite(s)

ellipsis, ellipses (pl)

elusive (evasive)

e-mail (E-mail in titles)

embargoes

embarkation

embarrass

embarrassment

embed

embellish

emigrant (going from)

emigre(s)

eminence grise

employee(s)

emptyhanded

encase

enclose

enclosure

encumber

encumbrance

encyclopedia

end date

endgain

endgame

end item, end-use item

endorse

endorsement

end use (n)

end-use (adj)

end user (n)

end-user (adj)

enforce

enforcement

enfranchise

engine-driven (um)

engine driver

enginehouse

engineroom

English-speaking (um)

en masse

ennui

enormity (great wickedness)

enormousness (n, great size)

enosis (**union**)

enroll, enrolled, enrolling, enrollment

en route

ensure (guarantee)

enterprise

entrench

entrepot(s)

entrepreneur

entrust

entry into force

entwine

envelop, enveloped, enveloping (v)

envelope (n)

environmental impact (um)

environmental protection (um)

environmental technology (um)

epilogue

equal, equaled, equaling, equality

equal rights (n, um)

Equator

equilibrium(s)

equip, equipped, equipping, equipment

erector-launcher

erratum, errata (pl)

error message (comp)

escapable

escudo(s)

ESDI (comp, Enhanced System Device Interface)

esprit de corps

esthetic

et al.

ethno (cf, usually one word)

Euro (cf, usually one word)

Euratom

euro, (currency of the EMU)

Eurocommunism

Eurodollar

Euroloan

European Central Bank (ECB)

European monetary union

European Union

Eurotunnel (Chunnel)

euro zone (n)

euro-zone (um)

evacuee

evenhanded

even-numbered (um)

ever-present (um)

everyday

ex

    ex cathedra

    excommunicate

    ex-Governor

    ex libris

    ex officio

    ex post facto

    ex rights

    ex-serviceman

    ex-trader

exceed

excel, excelled, excelling

exchange rate (um)

excise

ex-civil-servant (um)

Executive order (US President)

exercise

exhibitor

exhilarate

exhort

exonerate

exorbitant

exorcise

expediter

expel, expelled, expelling

export-control (um)

expose (v [two syllables], to lay open)

expose(s) (n [three syllables],
an exposure)

extant (in existence)

extol, extolled, extolling

extra (as pref, usually one word)

    extracurricular

    extra-heavy (um)

extra-large (um)

extra-long (um)

extramural

extraordinary

extraterritorial

extremely-low-frequency (adj)

eye-catching (um)

eyeglasses

eyeing

eye opener

eye-opening

eye to eye

eyewitness

facade (sing)

facedown (adj, adv, n)

face down (v)

face-off

face-saving (um)

face-to-face (adj)

factbook

factfinding

factsheet

Fahrenheit

fail-safe

fair-haired (um)

fairminded

fair-skinned (um)

fait accompli, faits accomplis (pl)

Falklands war

fall (season)

fallback (n, um)

fall guy

fallible

falloff (n)

fallout (n, um)

fall wheat

fan fold paper (comp)

faraway (um)

far cry

farfetched

farflung

far-left (adj), far-leftist (um)

farm bloc

farm-bred (um)

farmland

farmwork

farmworkers

far-reaching (um)

far-right (adj), far-rightist (um)

farseeing

farsighted

farther, farthest (physical or literal distance)

fast-breaking (um)

fast breeder reactor

fast-moving (um)

fast-newton reactor

fast-food (um)

fasttrack (v)

fast-track (adj)

father-in-law

fatwa

faultfinding

faultline

favor

fax (facsimile), faxed

fearmongering

feasible

featherbedding (n)

fedayee (sing rare), fedayeen

Federal Government (US only)

federal government (non-US)

feedback (n)

feedgrain

feedwheat

fellow traveler

fence jumper

fence-mending

fence-sitter

fence-sitting

ferro (cf)

    ferro-carbon-titanium

    ferro-uranium

    rest one word

ferryboat

fiascoes

fiber

fiberboard

fiberglass (unless trade name Fiberglas)

fiber-optic (adj)

fiber optics (n)

field day

field-deployed

field-grade (adj)

field grade (n)

field mark (comp)

fieldpiece

field-test (v)

fifth column

fighter-bomber

fighter-interceptor

fighter pilot (n, um)

fig leaf

figure 4 (reference)

figure eight

figurehead

file clerk

filmmaker, filmmaking

final assembly area

fine-tune (v)

fine-tuning

finger pointing (n)

fingerprint

fiord (as common noun: as part of name, follow capitalization decisions of cartographers in CPAS/CDPD)

firearm

fireball

firebomb, firebombed, firebombing

fire control (n)

fire-control (adj)

firecracker

fire drill (n, um)

firefight, firefighting, firefighter

fire-hardened (um)

firepower

fireproof

fire-resistant (um)

firesafe

fire storm

fire-support (adj)

firetruck

firewall (comp)

firewood

firm-handed (um)

first aid (n, um)

first-ballot (adj)

firstborn

first-class (adj)

first-come-first-served

first-echelon (adj)

first-half (adj)

firsthand (adv, um)

First Lady

firstline (adj)

first-named (um)

first-quarter (adj)

first-rate (adj)

first-stage (adj)

first-time (adj)

First World

fistfight

fit out, fitting out (v, gerund)

fitting-out (um)

fivefold

five-pointed (um)

Five-Year Plan (if specific)

fixed-rate (um)

fixed-wing (adj)

flagship (*but* American-flag ship)

flameproof

flamethrower

flammable (literal)

flareup (n)

flashpoint

flatbed (adj)

flatcar

flatfoot

flat-footed

flatout

flaunt (to display ostentatiously)

fledgling

flexible

flier

flight control (um)

flightcrew

flight deck

flight-hour

flightline

flightpath

flight test (n, adj)

flight-test, flight-testing (v, gerund)

flight time

flip-flop

Flogger B('s)

floodgate

floodlight

flood plain

floodwater

floor-length

floor plan

floorspace

flounder (to stumble about clumsily)

flout (to treat with contempt)

flow chart

fluorescent

fluoro (cf, all one word)

flyaway (adj)

flyover

FNU (first name unknown)

f.o.b. (free on board)

focus(es)

focus, focused, focusing

fold (suffix, usually one word)

    twofold

    fourfold

foldout

follow-on (n, um)

followthrough (n, um)

follow-up (n, um)

follow up (v)

foodgrain

foodgrower

food-processing (adj)

foodstore

foodstuffs

foolhardy

foolproof

foot-and-mouth (adj)

footbridge

foot-dragging

foothill

foothold

footnote (n, v)

foot-pound

footprint

foot soldier

footstep

forbade

forbear (v, tolerate)

forbid, forbade, forbidding

force majeure

forebear (n, ancestor)

forced labor

force-fed (adj)

forefront

forego (precede)

foregone conclusion

foreground (comp)

foreign decisionmaking

foreign exchange (n, um)

foreign-government-backed (um)

Foreign Military Sales

foreign policy making

Foreign Service

foremost

foresee

foreseeable

forestall

forest-covered (um)

forest land

foreword (prefatory note)

forgettable

forego (to precede in time or place)

forgo (do without)

forgone aid

forklift

format, formatted, formatting

formula(s)

forsake

forswear, forswore

forte

forthcoming

forthright

forthwith

FORTRAN (comp, formula translation)

fortuitous (happens by chance or accident)

fortune-teller

forum(s)

forward (adj, adv, opposite of backward)

forward-based (adj)

forward-looking (adj)

founder (to go lame, to collapse, to sink, to fail)

Four Power (adj)

Four Powers (n)

four-star (adj)

fourth-quarter (adj)

four-wheel drive (n)

four-wheel-drive (um)

framework

franchise

Francophone (n)

francophone (um)

Franco-Prussian War

fraught

free (suffix, usually hyphenated)

> **duty-free**
>
> **rent-free**
>
> *but* **carefree**

freedom fighter

free economic

free enterprise (n, um)

free-fall

free-for-all

freehand

freelance

freelancer

free market (n, um)

free-marketeer (n)

free-market-oriented (um)

free port

freer

free-spoken (um)

freestanding

freethinking

free trade (n, um)

free-trade-oriented

free up (comp)

freeway (highway)

freewheeling

free will (n)

freewill (adj)

freeze-drying

freight car

French Canadian (*but* **Italian-American, Chinese-American**)

French-English

French Revolutionary period

freshwater (um)

FROG

frogman

front burner

front-end (adj)

front-load (v)

front-loading (um)

frontline

front man

front page

frontrunner

frontrunning

frontseat

frost-free (um)

frostline

frostproof

fruitgrowing

FTP (comp, File Transfer Protocol)

fuel pump

full-blown

fullblooded

fullface

fulfill, fulfilled, fulfilling, fulfillment

full-fledged

full-grown (um)

full load

full-scale (um)

full-scope (um)

full-speed (adj, adv)

full-strength (adj, adv)

full-time (adj, adv)

fulsome (offensive to the senses or loathsome; it does not mean complete or full)

fundraiser, fundraising

funneled

funnel-shaped (um)

further, furthest (generally convey the notion of additional degree, time, or quantity)

fuse (preferred spelling except for missile and other military applications)

fuselage

fuze (certain military senses)

FY 2000

gainsay

gallbladder

Gambia (The) (n)

game plan

Gang of Four

gas-canister bomb

gas-driven (um)

gasfield (*but* oil and gas fields)

gas-fired (um)

gas-flow (adj)

gas-gathering (um)

gas-heated (um)

gas-laden (um)

gaslight

gasline

gas main

gas mask

gas oil

gastro (cf, usually one word)

gas well

gasworker

gasworks

gatekeeper

gauge

gazetteer

GDP (gross domestic product)

gearbox

gear-driven (um)

gearshift

gelcap

gendarme, gendarmerie (pl)

general counsels

general purpose (n, um)

gentlemen farmers

geopolitics

Germanys (reference)

ghettos

ghostwrite

ghostwriter

gibe (a taunt or sneer)

gigawatt-hour

give-and-take (n)

give away (v)

giveaway (n)

glamour (*but* glamorous)

glasnost

glassmaking

globetrotting

glove box

GmbH

GNP (gross national product)

go-ahead (n)

go-between(s) (n)

go-getter

going-on

gold mine

goodbye

good-faith (adj)

good-hearted (um)

good-heartedness

good-humored (um)

good offices

good-quality (adj)

good-to-excellent (um)

goodwill (salable asset, other economics senses)

good will (usually literal senses)

go-slow

Gosplan

gossiped-about (um)

gossipmonger

government-in-exile

governmentwide

governor(s) general

grab bag

graded earth runway

grainfield

grainland

grandstanding

grant(s)-in-aid

grapevine

grassroots (nonliteral)

gravesite (n)

gray

gray arms broker

gray arms market

gray-market (um, v)

great-aunt, great-uncle

Greater London, Greater Moscow

great-grandfather

Great Himalaya Range

great-power (adj)

greenbelt

greenhouse

grievous

ground attack (um, of aircraft)

ground-based (um)

groundbreaking

groundburst

ground-controlled (um)

ground crew

ground-effect machine (generic for Hovercraft vehicle)

ground fire

ground force (n, um)

ground forces (n, um)

ground-launched (um)

ground-mobile (um)

ground rules

ground station

ground support (um, of equipment)

ground swell

ground test (n, adj)

ground-test, ground-testing (v, gerund)

ground war

groundwater

groundwave

groundwork

groupware (comp)

growth rate

gruesome

G-7 summit

guarantee (n, v)

guaranty (n, used only in legal sense)

guardhouse

guerrilla

guesswork

guest worker

guidance and control (um)

guided-missile (adj)

guided-missile cruiser

guideline

guide rail

Gulf states (Persian)

Gulf war (Persian understood)

gun-barrel (adj)

gun battles

gunbearer

gun-bore (um)

gundeck

gunfighting

gunfire

gun-for-hire (n)

gunmaking

gunmen

gun mount

gunpoint

gunpowder

gunrunner

gunrunning

gunship

gunshot

gunsight

gun tube

gunsmith

Gypsies

habeas corpus (sing, pl)

Hague (The) (n)

hailstone

hailstorm

hairbreadth

hairline

hairsplitting

hajj(es) (Muslim pilgrimage)

hajji(s) (Muslim pilgrim, capitalize only if it precedes a person's name)

half brother

half-day (adj)

half-dozen (adj)

halfhearted

half hour

half-hourly (um)

half-life

half load

half-mast

half measure

half-mile (adj)

half-million (adj)

half-monthly (adj)

half moon

half-ripe (um)

half sister

half-speed (adj)

half-step

half-strength (adj)

halftime

halftrack

half-truth

halfway

half-yearly

Halley's comet

hallmark

ham-fisted

hamstring

hamstrung

handbook

hand-built (um)

hand-carry (v)

handclasp

handcuff(s)

hand-deliver (v)

handgrenade

handgun

hand-held (um)

hand-holding

handicap, handicapped, handicapping

hand-in-hand

handmade

hand-me-down(s) (n, adj)

hand off (v)

handoff (n, adj)

handout (n, um)

hand out (v)

hand-over (n)

handpicked

handrail

handshake

hands-off (adj)

hands-on (adj)

hand-wringing

handwritten

hangers-on

hang glider

hang-up (comp)

hangup (n)

harass

harbormaster

hard-and-fast

hardball

hard-charging (um)

hardcopy

hard core (n)

hard-core (adj)

hardcover

hard currency (n, um)

hard disk interface (comp)

hard-driving (um)

hardhat

hardheaded

hard-hit (um)

hard-hitting (um)

hard line (n)

hardline (adj)

hardliner (n)

hardnose

hard-nosed (adj)

hard-pressed (um)

hardstand

hard-target (adj)

hard up

hardware

hard-won (um)

hard work

hard-working (um)

harebrained

harvesttime

has-been (n)

Hatf (missile)

have-not (n, adj)

Hawk (aircraft)

    Blackhawk

    Jayhawk

    Nighthawk

    Oceanhawk

    Pavehawk

    Seahawk

HAWK (missile)

H-bomb

headfirst

headlight

headline

headlong

head-on (adj, adv)

headquarters

headrest

headroom

headstart

headstrong

head-to-head (um)

headwaters

headway

health-care (um)

healthful (producing health)

health worker

healthy (in good health)

heartbeat

heartland

heat-resistant (um)

heat-seeking (um)

heavy bomber (n, um, preferred by military)

heavy bomber base

heavy-duty (adj)

heavyhanded

heavy-lift (adj)

heavy-set (um)

heavy-water (adj)

heavy-water-moderated (um)

heavyweight (n, um)

hedgehop

height-finding (adj)

heir apparent

helicopter-borne (um)

hemisphere (but **Western Hemisphere**)

hemorrhage

Her Majesty's Government

hereafter

hereby

herein

heretofore

herewith

herself

heterogeneous

hexadecimal (comp)

heyday (n)

hidebound

hideout (n, um)

high-altitude (adj)

highborn

high-caliber (adj)

high-class (adj)

high-density (adj)

high-end (um)

high-energy (adj)

higher-income

higher-level (adj)

higher-paying

higher-ranking

higher-than-market price

higher-ups

highest-altitude (adj)

highest-ranking

high-explosive(s) (um)

high fidelity (n)

high-frequency (adj)

high-frequency direction-finding (um)

highhanded

high-intensity (um)

highland (n, um)

high-level (adj)

high light (literal)

highlight (nonliteral)

high-minded (um)

high point (literal, nonliteral)

high-power (adj)

high-precision (adj)

high-pressure (adj, v)

high-priced (um)

high-priority (adj)

high-profile (adj)

high-protein (adj)

high-quality (adj)

high-ranking (um)

high-resolution (adj, um)

high-rise (adj)

high school (n, um)

high-speed (adj)

high-strung (um)

high-tech(nology) (adj)

high-tension (adj)

high-value (adj)

high water mark

hijack

hijacker

hilltop

hill tribe

hindsight

hit-and-miss (adj)

hit-and-run (adj)

hit list

hit man

hit-or-miss (adj)

hodgepodge

hold off (v)

holdoff (n, adj)

holdout (n, adj)

holdover (n, adj)

hold time

holdup

Holocaust (the)

home bases

homebrew

homebuilding

home buyer

homecoming

home front

homegrown

home guard

homeland

homemade

homeowner

home page (comp)

home port (n)

home-port (v)

home rule

homesick

homestead

homestretch

hometown

homeward

homogeneous

honeycomb

honeymoon

Hong Kong government

honorbound

hookup (n, adj)

horrible

horseflesh

horselaugh

horseman

horseplay

horsepower

horserace

horseshoe

horsetrade (nonliteral)

horsetrading (nonliteral)

hostage taker

hostage taking

host-country (um)

host-government (um)

host-nation (um)

hotbed

hot-blooded (um)

hotheaded

hothouse

hot-launched

hotline (nonliteral)

hot-pursuit (adj)

hot-roll (v)

hotspot

hour-long

housebuilding

house call

house-clean (v)

housecleaner

house-cleaning (adj)

houseguest

household

housekeeping (*but* **safehouse keeper, safehouse keeping**)

houseowner (n)

housework

hover craft (unless trade name Hovercraft)

HTML (comp, HyperText Markup Language)

HTPB (hydroxyl-terminated polybutadiene

hull-less

human rights (n, um)

human-rights-related (um)

human-source (adj)

humdrum

hundredfold

hundredweight

hunger strike

hunker down (v)

hurly-burly

hush money

hushup (n, adj)

hydro (cf, usually one word)

   hydroelectric

   hydropower

hyper (pref)

   hyper-Dorian

   rest one word

   hyperlinks (comp)

   hypertext system (comp)

hypocrisy

hypothesis, hypotheses (pl)

I-beam

Iberian Peninsula

ibid.

iceberg

icebound

icebreaker

icecap

ice-covered (um)

ice cream

icefield

ice-free

icemaking

icepack

ice shelf

ice skate

ice-skate (v)

ice-skating

ice storm

IDE (comp, Integrated Drive Electronics)

idiosyncrasy

idyll

IF statement (comp)

Il-76 Candid

ill-advised (um)

ill-advisedly

illegible

ill-equipped (um)

ill health

illicit (illegal)

illiquid, illiquidity

ill-prepared (um)

ill-timed (um)

illusive (deceptive)

ill will

image-building (um)

image-enhancing (um)

image map (comp)

immersible

immigrant (coming into)

impasse

impel, impelled, impelling (to drive or urge by moral pressure)

impending (hint of threat or menace)

imperceptible

imperil, imperiled, imperiling

impermissible

impersuasible

implausible

implementer

imply (state something indirectly)

impossible

impostor

imprimatur

improvise

in absentia

inaccessible

inadmissible

inasmuch as

inaudible

inbound

in-board (adj)

inbox (n)

Inc.

incise

incompatible

incomprehensible

incontrovertible

incorrigible

incorruptible

in-country (adj, adv)

incredible

incur, incurred, incurring

indefensible

indelible

Independence Day

in-depth (um)

indestructible

indeterminate

index, indexes; indices (scientific only)

indications-and-warning intelligence

indict (to accuse)

indigestible

indite (to compose)

indivisible

Indo-European

industrywide

inedible

ineligible

inequity (unfairness)

inexhaustible

in extremis

infallible

infantryman

infeasible

infer (draw a conclusion or make a deduction), **inferred, inferring** (*but* **inferable, inference**)

infighter

infighting

inflammable (figurative)

inflexible

in-flight (um)

inflow

influence-buying (n)

information processing (comp)

infra (pref)

    infra-axillary

    infra-esophageal

    infra-umbilical

    rest one word

INF (intermediate-range nuclear forces) **talks**

INF Treaty

in-garrison

ingenious (skillful)

ingenuous (without guile)

in group (n)

in-house (adj, adv)

iniquity (sin)

ink jet (comp)

in-law (n)

inner-city (adj)

inner tube

innocuous

innuendo

inoculate

input (v)

inquire, inquired, inquiring

inquiry

inshore

insigne (sing rarely used), **insignia**

in situ

insofar as

inspectors general

install, installation, installed, installing, installment

instill, instilled, instilling

insure (cover by an insurance policy)

intangible

Intelink (comp)

Intelligence Community Staff

intelligence-gathering (um)

intelligentsia

intelligible

inter (pref, hyphened if second word is capitalized)

    inter-American

    inter-European

    rest one word

interactive processing (comp)

inter alia

intercede

interceptor

Interests Section

interface (comp)

interfere, interfered, interfering

interleaving (comp)

intermediate-range ballistic missile (IRBM)

intermediate-range nuclear forces (INF)

interment (burial)

intermittent

intern

Internet (comp)

internment (detention)

INTERPOL

interrepublic

interruptible

in-theater (um)

intifadah

in toto

intra (pref)

    intra-atomic

    intra-German

    rest one word

intransigent (n, adj)

intro (pref, all one word)

invincible

invisible

I/O (comp, input/output)

IP (comp, Internet Protocol)

ipso facto

Iran-Contra

Iran-Iraq war

irascible

IRBM (intermediate-range ballistic missile)

IRC (comp, Internet Relay Chat)

iridescence

ironclad

ironfisted

ironically (involves a sharp contrast between the apparent and the expected)

iron lung

ironmaking

ironworking

ironworks

irreducible

irreplaceable

irrepressible

irresistible

irresponsible

irreversible

Islamization

issues (are resolved, not solved)

iteration (comp)

its (possessive of it)

itself

jailbreak

Java (comp)

Javascript (comp)

jawbone

jerry-build (v)

jerry-built (um)

jet aircraft

jet airliner

jet bomber

jetliner

jet-powered (um)

jet-propelled (um)

jet propulsion

jet set

jibe (act of shifting sails)

jibe with (informally, agree)

jihad

jobholder

jobseeker

joint-service (adj)

joint-venture (adj)

journeyman

judgment

jukebox (n)

jumpoff (n, um)

jump off (v)

jump-start (n, v, adj)

jukebox (n)

jury-rigged (um)

just-completed (um)

kaleidoscopic

karaoke

keel-laying (um)

kerning (comp)

kerosene

ketchup (preferred catsup)

keypad (comp)

keyword

KGB/SVR (spans the service's conversion from KGB to SVR)

kickback (n, um)

kidnap, kidnapped, kidnapper, kidnapping

kidney stone

killjoy

kill rate

kilobyte (comp, KB)

kilo-class (um)

kilowatt-hour (kWh)

kimono(s)

kingmaker

kingpin

king-sized (um)

km/h (kilometers per hour)

knee-jerk (adj)

know-how (n, adj)

know-it-all (n, adj)

knowledgeable

know-nothing (n, adj)

Korean war

kowtow

Kresta-II(s)

kudos (*never* kudo)

label, labeled, labeler, labeling	**landward**
Labor Day	**landwire**
labor-intensive (um)	**laptop** (comp)
laborsaving	**large-scale** (adj)
labor union	**largess**
lackluster	**last-ditch** (adj)
laid-off (um)	**last-minute** (adj)
laid-up (participle)	**last-resort** (adj)
laissez-faire (n, adj)	**latecomer**
lakebed	**late-model** (adj)
lakefront	**late-night** (um)
lameduck (nonliteral)	**late-payments** (um)
LAN (comp, local area network)	**Latin American states**
Land, Laender	**latter-day** (adj)
land-attack (adj, of a missile)	**launch crew**
land base	**launch-on-tactical-warning** (n, adj)
land-based (um)	**launch on tactical warning** (v)
landborne	**launch-on-warning** (n, adj)
landbound	**launch on warning** (v)
land bridge	**launchpad**
landfill	**launch point**
landgrab	**launchsite** (*but* **space launch site**)
landholding	**launch stand**
landline	**launch weight**
landlocked	**law-abiding** (um)
landlord	**law-and-order** (adj)
landmass	**lawbreaker**
landmine	**lawsuit**
land-mobile (um)	**lawmaking**
landowner	**lay** (to put, place, or prepare and always takes a direct object), **laid, laid**
landownership	**laydown** (n, adj)
landowning	**layoff** (n, adj)
land-poor (um)	**layout** (n, adj)
Land Rover	**layover** (n, adj)
Landsat (US Earth resources satellite)	**layperson, laypeople**
landslide	**lay up** (v)
landstorm	**layup** (n, um)
land tax	**LCD** (comp, liquid crystal display)
land-use (um)	

lead-in (n, um)

leading edge (n)

leading-edge (um)

leadtime

lead up (v)

lead-up (n, um)

League of Nations

leakthrough

leapfrog

leap year

leather-bound (um)

leatherworking

Leclerc tank

lee shore

leeward

left-hand (adj)

left-leaning (adj)

left-of-center (um)

left wing (n)

leftwing (adj)

leftwinger

legible

legman

lend-lease

less (suffix, usually not hyphenated)

>   **dataless**

>   **weaponless**

>   *but* **hull-less**

>   **shell-less**

less developed (no hyphen)

lesser-known

less-than-even (um)

letter bomb

letter-perfect (um)

letterspacing

letterwriting

let up (v)

letup (n)

level, leveled, leveler, leveling

levelheaded

liaison

license

license plate (um)

Likud Party

lie (to recline or be situated and never takes a direct object) **lay, lain**

lifeblood

lifeboat

life cycle (n, um)

lifeguard

life insurance (n, um)

lifelike

lifeline

lifelong

liferaft

lifesaving

life-size (adj)

lifespan

lifestyle

lifetime

liftoff (n, um)

light bomber (um, preferred by military)

lighter-than-air craft

lighthearted

light-water (um, in reference to uranium)

light-water-reactor (um)

lightweight

light-year

like (suffix, usually one word)

>   **businesslike**

>   **lifelike**

>   *but* **bell-like**

>   **hull-like**

likable

likelihood

like-minded (um)

Likud bloc
linchpin
line-item (um)
line-of-sight (um)
line up (v)
line width
lineup (n, um)
link up (v)
links to
linkup (n, um)
lipservice
liquefy
liquid-propellant (adj)
liquid-propelled (um)
little-known (um)
little-used (um)
livedrop (nonliteral)
live-fire (um)
livewire (nonliteral)
living costs
llano(s)
Lloyd's (insurance)
Lloyds (bank)
LNU (last name unknown)
loadout
loan-sharking (n, um)
loath (adj, reluctant)
loathe (v, detest)
lock on (v)
lockon (n, adj)
lockout (n, um)
locus, loci (pl)
logbook
loggerheads
log in (comp)
logistic (adj)
logistics (n)
logjam
log on (comp)

London summit
lonely-hearts club
long ago (adv)
long-ago (um)
long-awaited (um)
long-bed (truck)
long-delayed (um)
long-distance (adj)
longest-ruling leader
long-lasting (um)
long-lived (um)
long-range (adj, *but* **Long Range Aviation** in Russia)
long-run (adj)
long shot (n)
long-shot (um)
long-sought
longstanding
long-term (adj)
longtime (adj)
long-winded
look-alike (n, adj)
lookdown/shootdown (um, of aircraft radar)
lookout (n, um)
loop (in the loop)
loophole
loose-knit (um)
looseleaf
loss-making (um)
lopsided
loudspeaker
low-altitude (um)
low-cost (um)
low Earth orbit (n)
low-Earth-orbit (adj)
lowercase
lower-class (adj)
lower-cost (adj)

lower-echelon (adj)

lower-grade (adj)

lower-house (adj)

lower house, upper house (um, in Japanese context)

lower-income (adj)

lower-level (adj)

lower-middle-class (adj)

low-flying (um)

low-frequency (adj)

low-income (adj)

low-key (adj, adv)

lowland (n, um)

low-level (adj)

low-light (um)

low-lying (um)

low-observable (n, adj)

low-paying (um)

low-power (adj)

low-pressure (um)

low-priced (um)

low-profile, lower-profile

low-quality (um)

Ltd.

lukewarm

lumberyard

lump-sum (um)

lunchtime

M.A.('s)

Maastricht Treaty

machine building (n)

machine-building (um)

machine dependent (comp)

machinegun

machine-made (um)

machine readable (comp)

machine shop

machine tool

machismo (n)

macho (adj)

macro (cf, all one word)

made-over (um)

made-up (um)

magnate (VIP)

magnet (metal attractor)

magnetos

mah-jongg

mail merge (comp)

mainframe (comp)

mainland

mainline (nonliteral)

main line (literal)

main memory (comp)

mainspring

mainstay

mainstream (nonliteral)

make-believe (n, adj)

makeshift

makeup (n, um)

make-work

mal (cf, all one word)

mala fide (adj, adv)

manageable

manager-director

man-day

maneuver

man-for-man

manhandle

manhole

man-hour

manic-depressive

manifold

man in the street

manmade (um)

man-of-war

manpack

man-portable (um)

manpower

mantel (shelf)

mantle (cloak)

man-year

many-sided (um)

mapmaker

mapreading

maquiladora

marijuana

market-oriented (um)

marketplace

marshal, marshaled, marshaling

mass-produce (v)

masterful (domineering, powerful)

masterly (knowledgeable, skillful)

mastermind

master's degree

master stroke

matrix, matrices

matter-of-fact (adj)

matter-of-factly (adv)

maxi (pref, all one word)

> *Note* that *maxi* can also be a separate word—noun or adjective

maximum, maximums

May Day (1 May)

mayday (distress call)

MBFR (mutual and balanced force reduction) **talks**

mea culpa

meager

mealtime

mean-spirited (um)

mean time (astronomical)

meantime (meanwhile)

meanwhile

meatpacking

media (always use pl)

Medicaid

Medicare

medieval

medium (sing rarely used), media

medium- and high-altitude (adj)

medium and high altitudes

medium bomber (um, preferred by
 military)

medium-size(d) (adj)

medium-to-high altitude (n)

medium-to-high-altitude (adj)

meetingplace

mega (cf, usually one word)

　　megabyte (comp, **MB**)

　　megadose

　　megaproject

member state (n)

member-state (adj)

mementos

memoir (personal reminiscence)

memorandum(s)

**Memorandum of Understanding
(MOU)**

menu driven (comp)

merchandise

merchantman

merchant ship

Mercosur

merged sort (comp)

messhall

messkit

mestizos

metal-coated (um)

metal-cutting (um)

metal-smelting

metalworker

metalworking

metamorphosis

metaphor (implied comparison of
dissimilar things)

meteorology

meter

Metro Manila

　　Metropolitan London

　　Metropolitan Moscow

　　but the Moscow metropolitan
　　area

micro (cf)

　　micro-organism

　　rest one word

mid (cf)

　　mid- and late 1990s

　　mid-April

　　midcareer

　　midday

　　mid-decade

　　mid-18th century (n)

　　mid-18th-century (adj)

　　mid-ice

　　midinfrared

　　midlevel

　　midmorning

　　mid-1960s-style (adj)

　　mid-1989

　　mid-1990s

　　mid-Pacific

　　midpoint

　　midsixties

　　midterm

　　midthirties

　　mid-to-late 1990s

　　mid-to-long-term (um)

　　midyear

middle age

middle-aged (um)

middle-class (adj)

Middle East (n, adj)

Middle Eastern (adj)

Middle East war

middle ground

middle-income (adj)

middle-level, midlevel (adj)

middleman

middle-of-the-roader

middle-size(d) (adj)

MiG-21 Fishbed

mild-mannered (um)

mileage

mile-long (adj)

milepost

milestone

mile-wide (adj)

milieu

military policymaking

militate (to have weight or effect, for or against)

militiaman

millennium, millennia (pl)

minable

mindreading

mind-set

mineclearing (um)

minefield

minehunters

minehunting

minelayer, minelaying

mineship

minesite

minesweeper, minesweeping

mine warfare (n, um)

mineworks

mini (pref, all one word)

>   miniempire

>   *but* mini-estate

>   *Note* that *mini* can also be a separate word—noun or adjective

minimum(s)

minimum-security (adj)

minister-counselor

minister-president

minuscule

minutes' (possessive case)

minutia (sing rarely used), minutiae

MIRVs (multiple independently targetable reentry vehicles)

>   unMIRVed

>   nonMIRVed

MIS (comp, management information system)

mischiefmaking

mischief-maker

missile-equipped (um)

missile-related (um)

missile support (n, um)

missile suspension (n, um)

Missile Technology Control Regime (MTCR)

Mission (UN)

misspell

mitigate (to moderate or alleviate)

mixup

mnemonics (comp)

mobile-erector-launcher (n)

mobile missile (n, um)

mockup (n)

Mod 4 (*but* modified HY-4)

model, modeled, modeler, modeling

modem (comp)

moderate-to-high (um)

modern-day (um)

modus operandi, modi operandi (pl)

modus vivendi, modi vivendi (pl)

mojahedin (Iran)

mold

Molotov cocktail

mommy track

money laundering (n)

money-laundering (um)

money-losing (um)

moneymaker

moneymaking

money market

moneys

moneysaving

monogram, monogrammed, monogramming

monologue

monthend

monthlong (adj)

month-old (adj)

months-long (adj)

moonlight

moonwalk

mop up (v)

mopup (n, um)

moratorium(s)

moreover

mosque (the)

most-favored-nation (adj)

most-sought-after (adj)

mothballed

mother-in-law

motherland

mother ship

motor torpedo boat

motorboat

motorcycle

motor-driven (um)

motorized rifle regiment

motorship

MOU (Memorandum of Understanding)

mountainside

mouthful

mouthpiece

movable

moviegoer

moviemaking

MRV (multiple reentry vehicle)

MTCR (Missile Technology Control Regime)

much-discussed (um)

much-needed (um)

muckrake (v)

muckraker (n)

mudbank

mudflat

mudslinging

Muhammad

mujahedin (Balkan/Bosnian context)

mujahidin (Arab countries and Afghanistan)

multi (cf, usually one word)

> multicolor
>
> multifiber
>
> *but* Multi-Fiber Arrangement (MFA)
>
> multi-ply (adj, several plies)
>
> multi-user system (comp)

multimillion-dollar (adj)

multiple independently targetable reentry vehicles (MIRVs)

multiple-purpose (um)

multiple reentry vehicles (MRVs)

multiple-restart

multiple rocket launcher

multiplexer (comp)

musclebound

music teacher

Muslim(s)

mutual and balanced force reduction (MBFR)

mutually agreed on

naivete

name-calling (um)

nameplate

Napoleonic code

narco (cf, all one word)
    narcoinsurgent
    Note that *narco* (sometimes just
    narc) can also be a separate word.
    Both the noun and especially the
    adjective should be limited to
    informal use.

narrowband (adj)

narrow-beam (adj)

narrow-body (n, adj, of aircraft)

narrow gauge (n)

narrow-gauge (um)

narrowminded

national-guard-type

nation-building

nation-states

nationwide

native-born (um)

natural gas

natural gas field

nearby

near-Earth orbit

near miss

near-real time (n)

near-real-time (adj)

near-record (um)

nearsighted

near success

near-term (um)

neck and neck

need-to-know

ne'er-do-well

negligible

neo (cf)
    neo-Communist
    neo-Nazi
    rest one word
    neocolonist

neofascist

nerve-racking

Netherlands (the) (n)

network

net worth

neuro (cf, all one word)

Neutral Zone

never-ending (um)

nevertheless

new-class missile (new class of missile)

newcomer

newfound

new-generation (um)

newly industrializing countries
(NICs) or economies (NIEs)

newsbroadcast

newscaster

news editor

news-gathering (um)

newsgroup (comp)

newsletter

newsmagazine

newsmaking

newspaper

newspaper reporter

newsprint

newsstand

newsweekly

news wire(s)

newsworthy

New Year (the)

New Year's Day

next-generation (adj)

next of kin

NIC (newly industrializing country)

nightclub

night editor

night-flying (um)

night letter

nightlong (um)

night school

night shift

nighttime

night-vision (um)

nightworker

Nile Delta

ninefold

nit-pick, nit-picking

NLQ (comp, near-letter quality)

Nobel prize

noblesse oblige

nobody

no-confidence (adj)

No Dong (missile)

no-fault (adj)

no-first-use (adj)

no-fly zone

noise-free

noisemaker

noisemaking

noisome (offensive and disgusting, like *a noisome odor*, or harmful)

no man's land

nom de guerre

nom(s) de plume

non (as prefix, usually one word)

nonaligned

Nonaligned Movement

Nonaligned summit

nonattributable

non-CIA

non-civil-service

noncontrol

nonetheless

non-European

nonferrous

nongovernmental organization (NGO)

non-intelligence-related

non-interest-bearing (um)

nonlifelike

nonMIRVed

non-missile-equipped

nonnuclear

non-nuclear-powered

non-nuclear-related

non-nuclear-weapon state

no-no, no-no's (pl)

no-nonsense (adj)

nonoceangoing

nonoil

non-oil-producing

non-party-member

non-Politburo-member

nonplused

non-printing character (comp)

nonproliferation

Non-Proliferation Treaty (NPT, spell out for first use)

non-rare-earth

nonrotating-Earth (um, extraterrestrial context)

non sequitur

nonuse-of-force (adj)

non-WEU-member

no one

northbound

north-central

northeast, northeastern

north end

Northern Atlantic continental shelf

northern-tier (um)

north-northeast

North Rhine–Westphalia

north shore

northward

North-West Frontier Province

nosecone

nosedive

no-show (n, adj)

notebook

note paper

noteworthy

noticeable

notwithstanding

nouveau riche, nouveaux riches (pl)

novel-writing (um)

no-war/no-peace

now-dominant (um)

nowhere

NTP (Non-Proliferation Treaty; Nuclear Non-Proliferation Treaty—spell out first time)

nuclear-armed (um)

nuclear-capable (um)

nuclear delivery (n, um)

nuclear-free (um)

Nuclear Non-Proliferation Treaty (NPT, spell out for first use)

nuclear power (n, um)

nuclear-powered (um)

nuclear-powered ballistic missile submarine (SSBN)

nuclear-related (um)

nuclear strike (n, um)

nuclear-war-fighting (um)

nuclear weapons (n, um)

nuclear-weapons-free (um)

nuclear-weapon-sized (um)

nuclear-weapons-related (um)

nuclear-weapon state

nucleus, nuclei

number-one, number-two (um)

oasis, oases (pl)

oblast(s)

occasional

occupied territory

occur, occurred, occurring

oceanborne

oceangoing

oceanside

oceanwide

OCR (comp, optical character recognition)

October War

odd number

odd-numbered (um)

OEM (comp, original equipment manufacturer)

off-and-on (um)

off-balance

off-base (um)

off-campus (um)

offcenter (um)

off chance

offcolor (um)

offday

off-duty (um)

offer, offered, offering

offguard

offhand

off-hours

officeholder

officer-in-alias

officers club

officeseeker

office-seeking (um)

officeworker

off-limits (um)

offline (um)

off line (pred)

off-load (v)

offloading

off-lying (um)

off-road

off-season

offset

offshoot

offshore

off-site

offstage

off-the-record (um)

off-the-shelf

off-track (*but* offtrack betting)

off year

oftentimes

oilfield (*but* oil and gas fields)

oil-processing (um)

oil-producing (um)

oil-rich

oil sands (n, um)

oilseed

oil shale (n, um)

oil slick

oilspill

oil-soaked (um)

oil well

oil workers

old-boys network

older-model (um)

old-fashioned (um)

old-guard (adj)

old-line (adj)

old-style

oldtime

Olympic Games

    Olympics

      Winter Olympics

      Summer Olympics

ombudsman, ombudsmen

on-again/off-again

on board (pred)

onboard (um, prep)

once-impressive

once-over

one-half

one-man (adj)

one-man/one-vote (n, adj)

one-on-one (adj, adv)

oneself

one-sided (um)

one-time (um, single instance)

onetime (um, former)

one-up

one-upmanship

one-way

ongoing

on line (pred)

online (um)

only-child complex

on-screen

onshore

on-site (um)

on-station (um)

onstream (um)

on-the-job training

on-time (um)

OPEC summit

open-air (um)

open-door (um)

open-ended (um)

openhanded

open-heart (adj)

open-market

openminded

open-ocean (adj)

open pit (n, um)

open-sea (um)

open-source (adj)

opium poppy field (*but* poppyfield)

opium poppy growing area

optic-fiber (um)

optoelectronics

orbit, orbital, orbited, orbiter, orbiting

order-of-battle (um)

ordinance (law)

ordnance (weapons)

orthodox

ostensible

ourselves

out (prefix, one word)

outermost

outfit, outfitted, outfitter, outfitting

outmigration

outnumbered

out-of-area (um)

out-of-date (um)

out-of-pocket (um)

out-of-touch (um)

over (cf, one word)
   (*exception*: over-snow vehicle)

overflow (comp)

overhead (all senses)

overland radar

overlap, overlapping, overlapped

overnight

overreaching

overreact

overstaff

overwrite (comp)

ozone-depleting (um)

pacemaker

pace-setting (um)

Pacific Rim

page proof

painstaking

palate (roof of mouth)

palisade

pallet (bed, platform)

pan (cf, one word except with uppercase words, and then uppercase P)

    panchromatic

    pannational

    pantheism

    Pan-American

    Pan-Slavic

panic buying

papacy

papal

papermaker, papermaking

papermill

paperwork

paragraph 12

parallel, paralleled, paralleling

parallel processing (comp)

paralysis (n)

paralyze (v)

paraphernalia

parastatal (state administered—Third World)

parcel, parceled, parceling

parenthesis, parentheses (pl)

par excellence

Paris accords

parkland

particle beam weapon

part owner

part-time (adv, um)

part way

party giver

party goer

party line

partywide

passageway

passenger car

passer(s)-by

passport

pass through (v)

passthrough (n, adj)

password

past-due (um)

pastureland

pathbreaker

pathfinder

patrol, patrolled, patrolling

payback (n)

paycheck

payload

pay off (v)

payoff (n, um)

payroll

PDA (comp, personal digital assistant)

PDL (comp, page description language)

peacekeeping

peace-loving (um)

peacemaking

peace talks

peacetime

pedal, pedaled, pedaling

P-8 meetings

pending (yet to come or not yet settled)

peninsulawide

pen name

pent-up (um)

peptalk

per capita

percent

percentage

percentile

perceptible

per diem

peremptory

perestroyka

perl (comp, Practical Extraction and Report Language)

permafrost

Permanent Representative to the United Nations

Perm Five (in UNSC)

permissible

permit, permitted, permitting

perquisite (privilege)

per se

Persian Gulf states

Persian Gulf war (Gulf war)

Pershing Ia('s), *but* **Pershing II(s)**

persistent

personal (of the individual)

persona non grata, personae non gratae (pl)

personnel (staff)

perspective (view)

persuasible

petro (cf)

    petro-occipital

    rest one word

    petrodollars

phased-array (adj)

phase down (v)

phasedown (n, um)

phase in (v)

phasein (n, um)

phase out (v)

phaseout (n, um)

Ph.D.('s)

phenomenon, phenomena (pl)

Philippines (the) (n)

phone-in (um)

photo (cf)

    photo atlas

    photo-offset

    photo-oxidation

    rest one word

photocopies

photomap

photoreconnaissance satellite

PhotoCD (comp)

picayune

picket line

pick-me-ups

pickpocket

pick up (v)

pickup (n, adj)

picnicking

piece goods

piecemeal

piece rate

piecework(er)

piggyback

piledriver

PIM (comp, personal information manager)

pinstripe

pipe bomb

pipedream

pipefitting

pipelaying

pipeline

pipe smoker

pixel (comp)

place name

plainclothes

plainclothesman

plain-spoken (um)

plaintext

planeload

plantlife

plaster of Paris

plateau(s)

plate glass

plausible

plea bargain (n)

plea-bargain (um)

plenum

PLO chairman

plowshare

plug-in (n, adj)

plus or minus

p.m.

pock-marked (um)

pointblank

point man

police (always plural)

policymaker, policymaking (spell as two words when accompanying adjective modifies only policy as in **economic policy maker**—*but* **unauthorized policymaking**)

politicking

politico (cf)

    politico-orthodox

    rest one word

pollwatcher

poor-quality (adj)

poppyfield (*but* opium poppy field)

poppy growing (um)

poppyseed

popular-front (um)

populate (comp, v)

popup (n, um)

pork-barrel (adj)

portentous

porthole

portside

possible

post

    post bellum

    post-civil-war (um)

    post office

    post-target-tracking

    as prefix, generally one word

    postattack

    postboost

    postcoup

    postgraduate

posthaste

postmortem

postreentry

posttest

posttreatment

posttreaty

postcard (n)

PostScript (comp)

pot-banging (um)

potbellied

potboiler

potluck

potpourri

potshot

poultryman

poultry-raising (um)

poverty-stricken

power base

power breakfast

power broker

power-driven (um)

power-generating

power grab

power grid

powerhouse

powerline

PowerPC (comp)

power plant

power play

PowerPoint (comp)

power-projection (um)

power sharing (n)

power-sharing (um)

powersharing (v)

power station

PPP (comp, Point-to-Point Protocol)

practice (n, v)

praiseworthiness

praiseworthy

pre (pref)
    pre-flight-test (um)
    pre-Incan
    pre-position (v, position in advance)
    pre-martial-law
    rest one word
    predetente
    preelection
    preexisting
    preindependence
    prewar
precede (be ahead of)
precedence (priority)
precedents (prior instances)
precis (sing, pl)
precision-guided missile (PGM)
predilection
predominant (adj)
predominate (v)
preempt
prefectible
prefer, preferred, preferring (*but* **preferable, preference**)
prerequisite (need)
present-day (um)
president-elect
presidential (non-US)
Presidential (US—past or present)
presidential guard
president(s)-elect
press agent
press-gang (n, v)
presstime
pressure-cooker bomb
prevaricate
price-sharing (um)
prima donna behavior
prima facie
prime minister

prime-minister-designate (general sense)
    but the **Prime Minister–designate**
prime-ministerial
prime-ministership
prime-ministry
prime mover
prime-time (um)
principal (sum of money, chief)
principle (proposition)
printout
printshop
prisoner of war (n)
prisoner-of-war (um)
private-sector (um)
privilege
prizewinner, prizewinning
    but **Nobel Prize winner**
pro
    pro-African
    pro-arms-control (um)
    pro forma
    pro-free-market (um)
    pro-free-trade
    pro rata
    pro-state
    pro tem
    pro tempore
    pro-vice-regent
    as prefix, generally one word
    proactive
    proapartheid
    progovernment
    proreform
    proregime
    proruling
    prowar
problem-solving (um)
proceed (move ahead)
processible

producible

production-sharing (um)

profederal

proffer, proffered, proffering

profit, profitable, profited, profiting

profit-and-loss (um)

profitmaking

profit-sharing (um)

program, programmed, programmer, programming, programmable, programmatic

prologue

proofread

proofroom

propel, propellant, propelled, propeller, propelling (to drive or urge by a force that imparts motion)

prophecy (n)

prophesy (v)

propjet

prospective (expected)

protege(s)

protester

protocol

proved (v, adj, for energy reserves only)

proven (adj, except energy reserves)

proviso(s)

pseudo (cf)

    pseudo-Messiah

    pseudo-official

    pseudo-peace-loving

    rest one word

publicity-conscious (um)

public-sector (um)

public-spirited (um)

public works

pullback (n, um)

pullout (n, um)

pulsed Doppler effect

pulse-Doppler

pulsewidth

pummel, pummeled, pummeling

pump house

pump-priming (adj)

pump station

purse strings

pushover (n, um)

pushup (n, um)

put-on (n, um)

put-up (n, um)

quality-of-life (um)

quarrel, quarreled, quarreling

quarterdeck

quartermaster

quadripartite

quasi (pref, all hyphened)

> *Note* that *quasi* can also be a separate adj

quasi currency board

Quebecer

Quebecois

questionnaire

queue

quick-count polling

quick fix

quick-reaction (adj)

quicksilver

quick time

quick-witted (um)

quid pro quo(s)

quitclaim

rabble-rouser

racehorse

racetrack

rack (framework)

radar-absorbing (um)

radar-cross-section

radar tracking

radio

    radio amplifier

    radio antenna

    radio-cassette

    radio channel

    radio communication(s)

    radio control

    radio engineer

    radio engineering

    radio link

    radio navigation

    radio-paging (um)

    radio range

    radio receiver

    radio relay

    radio set

    radio station

    radio transmitter

    radio tube

    radio wave

    as combing form, one word

    radioactive

    radiobroadcast

    radioelectronic

    radiofrequency

    radioisotope

    radiotelegraph

    radiotelephone

Radio Free Asia

radius, radii

rag-tag

railborne

railcar

railhead

rail line

rail-mobile (um)

rail net

railroad

railroader

rail shed

rail spur

rail train

railway

railwayman

railyard

raincheck

rainfall

rain-fed (um)

rain forest

rainmaking

rainproof

rainshower

rainspout

rainstorm

raintight

rainwater

raison(s) d'etre

RAM (comp, random-access memory, read/write memory)

Ramadan

ramjet

ramrod

ramshackle

rangefinder

rangehead

range rate (n)

range-rate (adj)

rank and file (n)

rank-and-file (adj)

rank and filer (n)

rapid fire

rapid transit

rapid-reaction (um)

rapid-response (um)

rapporteur(s)

rapprochement

rare-earth (um)

rate-cutting (um)

rate-fixing (um)

ratesetting

rat-infested (um)

ratline

rat race

raveling

raykom(s)

rayon(s)

razor-sharp (um)

re (pref)

    re-cover (cover again)

    re-create (create again)

    re-cross-examination

    re-direct

    re-form (form again)

    re-ice

    re-ignite

    re-ink

    re-instate (instate again)

    re-invent

    re-present (present again)

    re-redirect

    re-treat (treat again)

    rest one word

    realign

    reestablish

    reman

read-only (comp)

readout (n)

read/write (comp)

ready-built (um)

readymade

ready reference

real estate (n, um)

realpolotik

real-time (adj)

rear area (um)

rear end

rear-guard (adj)

rear service

rear services area

rebel, rebelled, rebelling

rebut (to argue to the contrary)

recently designed logo

receptible

reckless

reconnaissance

reconnoiter

recordbreaking

recordkeeping

recordmaking

red, redder, reddened, reddening

red-blooded (um)

red-carpet (um)

red-haired (um)

redhanded

redhead, redheaded

red-hot (um)

redound

red tape (literal)

redtape (nonliteral)

reduced-observable (n, adj)

reducible

reemerge

reenter

reentry

reequip

reevaluate

reexport

refer, referred, referring (*but* referable, reference)

referee

referendum(s)

reformat

reform-minded

refuel, refueled, refueling

refusenik

refute (connotes success in winning the argument)

regionwide

reign (to exercise sovereign power)

rein (to guide, control, or hold back)

reinforce

relations with

relay chat (comp)

relevant

reluctant (unwilling to act)

reminiscent

remit, remitted, remitting

remote-control (um)

remote-controlled

remote-sensing (um)

renaissance (*but* the **Renaissance**)

Renaissance man

rent-free

repairman

replication (comp)

reprehensible

Representative (US Congress)

representative at large

representative-elect

reprocess

republicwide

requester

research study

Resident (diplomatic)

residences

resilient

resistant

responsible

rest cure

rest home

restroom

resume(s)

reticent (uncommunicative or reserved)

retrofire

retrofit

retrorocket

reuse

Reuters (news agency)

reverse-engineer, reverse-engineering, reverse-engineered

reversible

revise

Revolutionary Guard (force or members)

ricefield

ricegrowing

riceland

ridge line

rifleman

right-angled (um)

right away

right-hand (adj)

right-handed (um)

right-of-way, rights-of-way

right-to-work (adj)

right turn

right wing (n)

rightwing (adj)

rightwinger

ringleader

ring-shaped (um)

ringside

ringworm

riot-control (um)

riptide

rise

risk taking, risk taker

rival, rivaled, rivaling

riverbank

riverbed

riverborne

river bottom

river-crossing

riverfront

riverside

r/min (revolutions per minute)

roadbed

roadblock

roadbuilding

road-clearing (um)

roadmap

road-mobile (um)

road scraper

road show

roadside

road-test (v)

roadway

road-weary (um)

rob, robbed, robber, robbing

rockbottom (nonliteral)

rockslide

rock wool

rogue states

rollback (n, um)

rollcall

rolling-stock (adj)

roll-on/roll-off (um, of ships)

    Ro/Ro (military) or **ro/ro**

rollout (n, um)

rollout-to-launch (um, of weapons)

rollover (n, um)

roll-up (n, um)

roll up (v)

ROM (comp, read-only memory)

rooftop

rough-and-ready (um)

rough-and-tumble (n, adj)

roughcast (um, v)

rough-faced (um)

roughhewn

roughhouse

roughneck

roughrider

rough-sketch (v)

roundabout (n, um)

roundrobin (petition)

roundtable (panel)

round-the-clock

round-topped

round trip (n, um)

round up (v)

roundup (n, um)

rowboat

rubberband

rubbernecker

rubber plant

rubber stamp (literal, n)

rubberstamp (nonliteral, n, um, v)

rubber-stamped (literal, um)

rubles' (pl possessive case)

rulemaking

rule of thumb

rules-of-origin

ruling-family (adj)

ruling-party (adj)

rumormonger

run

    runaround (n, adj)

    runaway (n, adj)

    rundown (n, um)

    run in (v)

    run-in (n, um)

    runoff (n, um)

    runthrough (n, um)

    runup (n, um)

    run up (v)

    runway

runner-up

running mate

run time (comp)

rush hour

Russian Far East

rustproofing

rust-resistant (um)

saber rattling (n)

saber-rattling (um)

saddle stitch (n)

saddle-stitch (v)

saddle-stitched (um)

safe-conduct (n, adj)

safecracking

safe-deposit (adj)

safeguard

safehaven

safehouse

safehouse keeper, safehouse keeping

safekeeping

sailboat

sailcloth

sailmaking

SAL (strategic arms limitations)

salable

salesclerk

salesmanship

salesperson, salespeople

sales tax

SALT (strategic arms limitation talks)

salt flat

saltwater

samizdat

samurai

San Andreas Fault

sanatorium(s)

sandbag

sandbank

sandbar

sandblast

sand dune

Sandinista

sandpaper

sandstorm

sandy-bottomed (um)

sanguinary (bloodthirsty)

sanguine (ruddy or optimistic and cheerful)

sanitarium(s)

sans serif

satellite

satellite-borne (um)

Saudi Arabia (or the Kingdom)

sawmill

saw-toothed (um)

say-so (n)

scale up (v)

scaleup (n)

scaling back

scandalmongering

scapegoat

scarce

scaremonger

scareproof

scatterbrained

scene setter

school-age (adj)

school board

schoolbook

schoolboy

schoolbus

schoolchildren

schoolday

schoolgirl

schoolgrounds

schoolhouse

schoolroom

schools of thought

schoolteacher

    but high school teacher

school-trained (um)

schoolwork

schoolyard

school year

scoreboard

scorecard

scorekeeping

scot-free

Scotsman

scout car

scrapbook

scrap heap

scrap iron

scrap paper

scrapyard

scratch pad

scratch test

screen blanker (comp)

screenplay

screen saver (comp)

screenwriter

screw-driven (um)

screwdriver

screw propeller

screw-threaded (um)

screw wheel

scrolling (comp)

scrubland

SCSI (comp, Small Computer System Interface)

scuba

Scud B('s)

scuttlebutt

SDI (Strategic Defense Industry)

sea

    sea-based (um)

    seabed

    seaboard

    seaborne

    seacoast

    seacraft

    seafaring

    seafloor

    seafood

    seagoing

    seakeeping

    sea lane

    sea-launched cruise missile (SLCM)

sea level

sea life

sealift

sea lines of communication (SLOC)

sea lion

seaplane

seaport

seapower

sea route

seashore

seasick

seaside

sea test

seawall

seaward

seawater

seaway

seaworthy

search-and-destroy (um)

search engine (comp)

searchlight

searchplane

seatbelt

second-best (adj)

second-class (adj)

second-degree (adj)

second-generation (adj)

second-guess (v)

second-half (adj)

second hand (n)

secondhand (adv, adj)

secondhand smoke

second in command

second-largest (adj)

second-leading (um)

second-most-powerful (um)

    but secondmost

second-quarter (adj)

second-ranking (um)

second-rate

second-rater

second-tier (um)

Second World War

secretary general, secretaries general

secretary-generalcy

secretary-generalship

secretaryship

secretary-treasurer

secret service

secret society

secretwriting

security decisionmaking

seesaw

seize

self (reflexive prefix, use hyphen)

    self-motivated

    self-trained

(reflexive pronoun, omit hyphen)

    myself

    yourself

selfless

selfsame

sell off (v)

selloff (n, adj)

sellout (n, um)

semi (pref)

    semi-armor-piercing

    semi-Christian

    semi-idleness

    semi-independent

    semi-indirect

    semi-land-mobile

    semi-winter-hardy

    rest one word

    semiannual

    semiarid

    semidesert

    semiofficial

    semiweekly (twice a week)

Senator (US Congress)

sendoff (n, um)

separate

Serbo-Croatian

serious-minded (um)

serviceable

service-connected (um)

serviceman

servicewide

servomechanism

set back (v)

setback (n, um)

set down (v)

setdown (n, um)

set in (v)

set-in (n, um)

set off (v)

setoff (n, um)

setpiece

set-to (n, um)

set up (v)

setup (n, um)

sevenfold

severalfold

SGML (comp, Standard Generalized Markup Language)

shadowbox (v)

shake down (v)

shakedown (n, adj)

shake out (v)

shakeout (n. adj)

shake up (v)

shakeup (n, adj)

shallow-draft (adj)

shamefaced

shameworthy

shantytown

shaped-charge (adj, of warheads)

sharecropper

shareholder

shareware (comp)

sharp-angled (um)

sharp-edged (um)

sharpshooting

sharp-witted (um)

shaykh

sheep farm

sheepherder, sheepherding

sheepkeeping

sheepland

sheepshearing

sheepskin

sheet metal

shelf life

shelf plate

shellburst

shellfish

shell game

shellhole

shell-like

shellproof

shellshocked

sherpa

shilly-shally

ship (suffix, usually one word)

    partnership

    premiership

    prime-ministership

shipboard

shipborne

shipbuilders

shipbuilding

ship-day

shipload

shipowner, shipowning

shipshape

shipwrecked

shipyard

shock wave

shogun

shoo-in

shoot down (v)

shootdown (n)

shootout

shopkeeping

shoplifting

shopowner

shoptalk

shopworn

shoreland

shore leave

shoreline

shortchange (v)

short circuit (n)

short-circuit (v)

short-circuited (um)

shortcoming

shortcut (n, adj, v)

shortfall

shorthand (writing)

short-handed (um)

short-lived (um)

short-range (adj)

short run (n)

shortrun (adj)

shortsighted

short-term (adj)

short-to-long (adj)

short-to-long-range (adj)

short ton

shortwave (radio)

shogun

shoulder-launched (um)

showcase

showdown

showman

showoff (n, um)

showpiece

shura

shutdown (n, um)

shut down (v)

shut-in (n, um)

shutoff (n, um)

shutout (n, um)

[*sic*]

sickbay

sickbed

sick leave

sidearms

side effect

side line (literal)

sideline (nonliteral)

side lobe

side road

side-scan radar

sideshow

sidestep

sideswipe

sidetrack

sidetrip

sidewalk

sideways

siege

sightreading

sightsaving

sightseeing

signal, signaled, signaler, signaling

signalman

signal-processing (um)

signal tower

SIGINT

signoff (n, um)

sign-on (n, um)

signpost

signup (n, um)

SII (Structural Impediments Initiative)

silk screen

silkworm

silo-based (um)

silver-gray (um)

silver-haired (um)

silver-tongued (um)

silverware

silverworker

simon-pure (um)

simple-minded (um)

simple-witted (um)

simulcast

sine qua non(s)

single-handed (um)

single-handedly (adv)

single-minded (um)

single-mindedly (adv)

single-mindedness (n)

single-most-important (um)

single-seat (um)

single-source (um)

single-track (adj)

single warhead

Sino- (as prefix)

siphon

sister(s)-in-law

sit com

sitdown (n, um)

sit in (v)

sit-in (n, um)

Six-Day War

sizable

skied, skiing

skillful

skindeep

skinhead

skyjack, skyjacker

skylight

skyline

skyrocket

skyscraper

skyward

skywriting

slaughterhouse

slaveholding

slaveowner

slave trade

SLBM (submarine-launched ballistic missile)

SLCM (sea-launched cruise missile)

sledge hammer

sleepwalking

sleetstorm

slide rule

SLIP (comp, Serial Line Internet Protocol)

slip-up (n, um)

SLOC (sea lines of communication)

slowdown (n, um)

slowgoing

slow-motion (adj)

slow-moving (um)

slowpoke

slow time

slowup (n, um)

slow-witted (um)

sluice gate

slumdweller

slumlord

small arms (n)

small-arms (adj)

small business

small businessman

smallpox

small-scale (adj)

smalltalk

small-time, small-timer

small-to-moderate (um)

smalltown (um)

small-unit (adj)

smart aleck

smart-alecky (um)

smart-looking (um)

smart set

smashup (n, um)

smear culture

smokebomb

smoke-filled (um)

smokeproof

smokescreen

smokestack

smolder

smoothbore

smooth-tongued (um)

smooth-working (um)

smudge pot

snail-paced

snail-slow (um)

snail's pace

snowball

snowbank

snowbound

snowcapped

snow cover

snow-covered (um)

snowcraft

snowdrift

snowfall

snowline

snowmobile

snowshoe

snowstorm

snow-topped (um)

snow-white (um)

so

    so-and-so

    so-called (um)

    so-seeming (um)

    so-so

soapbox

soap opera

sober-minded (um)

sobersided

sobersides

sob sister

sob story

social work(er)

socio (cf)

    socio-official

    rest one word

    socioeconomic

soft coal

soft copy (n)

soft-copy (adj)

soft drink (n, um)

soft goods

softhearted

soft-pedal (v)

soft-soap (v, nonliteral)

soft-soaped

soft-spoken (um)

software

Solidarity (Poland)

solid-propellant (adj)

solid rocket propellant

solid-state (adj)

solo(s)

some

    somebody

    someday

    somehow

    someone (anyone)

    some one (distributive)

    someplace (adv)

    something

    some time (n, an unspecified time)

    sometime (adj, occasional; adv, at an unspecified time)

    sometimes (adv, occasionally)

    somewhat

    somewhere

son(s)-in-law

sonobuoy

soon-to-be- (um, often prefixed)

sore point

sorry-looking (um)

soulmate

soul-searching (um)

sound-absorbing (um)

soundingboard

sound-minded (um)

soundoff (n, um)

soundproof

sound wave

sourfaced

sour grapes

sour-natured (um)

sous-sherpa

southbound

south-central

southeast

southeast-bound (um)

south end

Southern Tier

south side

south-southeast

southward

southwest

Soviet Bloc

soybean

space age

space-based (um)

spaceborne

spacecraft

spaceflight

space key

space launch site (n, um)

space mine

space plane

spaceship

space station

space suit

space tracking (n, um)

space walk

Spanish American

Spanish-born (um)

Spanish-speaking (um)

spare-parts (adj)

spark plug

sparse

special envoy

special-forces (adj)

special-interest (adj)

special-purpose (adj)

Special Weapons and Tactics (SWAT)

specter

spectrum, spectra (pl)

speechwriter, speechwriting

speedboat

speed up (v)

speedup (n, um)

speedwriting

spellbind, spellbinder, spellbinding, spellbound

spell checker (comp)

spendthrift

spent-fuel (adj)

spent nuclear fuel reprocessing plant

Spetsnaz

spill over (v)

spillover (n, um)

spillway

spin control

spin off (v)

spinoff (n, um)

spin up (v)

spinup (n, um)

splash down (v)

splashdown (n, um)

split second

splitup (n, um)

spoilsport

spokesperson

sports bar

sportsmanlike

spot check (n)

spot-check (v)

spreadsheet

spring (season)

springboard

spring fever

springtime

spur line

square-bottomed (um)

square deal

square meter

square root

squeeze play

SRF (Strategic Rocket Forces)

SS-7(s)

SSB (ballistic missile submarine)

SSBN (nuclear-powered ballistic missile submarine)

SS-N-4(s)

S&T (science and technology)

stadium(s)

stage-manage, stage-managing

stairstep

stalemate

stalking-horse (n)

stanch (v, stop)

stand alone (v)

stand-alone (n, adj)

standard bearer

standard gauge (n)

standard-gauge (adj)

standard time

standback analysis

standby (n, um)

stand by (v)

stand down (v)

standdown (n, um)

stand fast (v)

standfast (n, um)

stand in (v)

stand-in (n, um)

standing-room-only (um)

standoff (n, adj)

stand off (v)

standoffish

stand out (v)

standout (n, um)

stand pat (v)

standpat (n)

standpatter

standpoint

standstill (n, um)

stand still (v)

stand up (v)

standup (n, um)

starboard

STARS (comp, Storage Archive and Retrieval System)

star-spangled (um)

START (strategic arms reduction talks) **Treaty**

start up (v)

startup (n, um)

Stasi (former East German Secret Police)

state banking system

state enterprise industrial sector

state enterprise sector

statehood

state of the art (n)

state-of-the-art (adj)

state of the union

state of war (n)

state-of-war (adj)

State Planning Committee (Gosplan)

stateroom

state-run (um)

statesman

statesmanlike

stateswoman

statewide

stationary (fixed)

stationery (paper)

stationmaster

station wagon

Status of Forces Agreement (SOFA)

status quo

statute book

statute mile

staunch (adj, steadfast)

stay-at-home (n, adj)

stayaway

staybehind (n)

stealth

stealth bomber

stealth technology

steamboat

steam-driven (um)

steam engine

steamer-borne (um)

steamer line

steamfitting

steam heat

steampipe

steam-propelled (um)

steamroller (n, um, v)

steamship

steelhearted

steelmaking

steel mill

steel-producing (um)

steel trading

steel wool

steelworker

steelworks

stepbrother, stepchild

steppingstone

step up (v)

step-up (n, um)

stick-in-the-mud (nonliteral)

stick-to-it-iveness

stillborn

still life

still-lingering (um)

still-to-be- (um, often prefixed)

still-unseated (um)

stimulus, stimuli (pl)

stockholder
stock-in-trade
stock market (n, um)
stockpile
stockraising
stock-still (um)
stocktaking
stockyard
stone-cold (um)
stonecutting
stone-deaf (um)
stonehearted
stone wall (n)
stonewall (v, nonliteral)
stopgap
stoplight
stopoff (n, adj)
stop off (v)
stop over (v)
stopover (n, adj)
stopwatch
storefront
storeowner
storm-swept (um)
storytelling
storywriting
stouthearted
stow away (v)
stowaway (n, um)
straightaway
straight face
straight-faced (um)
straightforward
straitjacket
straitlaced
straight line
straight-spoken (um)
stranglehold
straphanger
strap on (v)

strap-on (n, adj)
stratagem
strategic arms limitations (SAL)
strategic arms limitations talks (SALT)
strategic arms reduction talks (START)
Strategic Rocket Forces (SRF)
stratum, strata (pl)
strawman (nonliteral)
straw vote
streambed
streamline, streamlined
streetcar
streetsmart
streetwise
stretchout (n, um)
strikebreaker
strikeout (n, um)
strikeover (n, um)
strong-arm (um, v)
strongbox
stronghearted
stronghold
strongman (nonliteral)
strong-minded (um)
strong point (personal forte)
strongpoint (military fortification)
strong-willed (um)
stubbornness
stumblingblock
stupid-looking (um)
stylebook
style guide
style manual
Su-20 Fitter
sub
    sub-Himalayan
    sub rosa
    Sub-Saharan

sub-subcommittee

rest one word

subbalance

subbasement

subbasin

subchaser

subcommittee

subcontinental

submachinegun

submarginal

subpolar

substandard

subsystem

subunit

submarine-launched ballistic missile (SLBM)

submit, submitted

subpoena

subtlety

succeed

sudden-death (um)

sugar beet

sugarcane

sugar-coat (v)

sugar-coated (um)

sugar mill

sulfur (derivatives also spelled with f)

summer (season)

summer school

summertime

summit (OPEC)

sundown

sun-dried (um)

sunlit

sunrise

sunset

sunshine

sunstroke

suntan

sunup

super (*note* that *super* can also be a separate word—n, or, informally, adj or adv)

super-Christian

super-high-frequency

super-superlative

rest one word

superegoist

superhighway

supermarket

superpower

supersede

supervise

supra (pref)

supra-abdominal

supra-Christian

rest one word

supranational

suprarenal

sure-fire (adj)

sure-footed (um)

sure thing

surface-burst (adj)

surface ship (n, um)

surge protector (comp)

surmise

surprise

surreptitious

surveil, surveilled, surveilling, surveillance

susceptible

SWAT (Special Weapons and Tactics)

sweepstake

swellhead

sweptback (n, um)

sweptwing (n, um)

swing shift

swingwing

switchblade

switchboard

switch box

switch over (v)

switchover (n)

switch tower

switchyard

syllabus(es)

symposium(s)

synonymous

synopsis, synopses (pl)

synthetic-aperture (adj, of radar)

syrup

system backup (comp)

table A-4

tableau(s)

taboo

tailgate

tailormade

tailpipe

tailspin

Taiwan (n, adj)

take down (v)

takedown (n, adj)

take home (v)

take-home (n, adj)

take off (v)

takeoff (n, adj)

take out (v)

takeout (n, adj)

take over (v)

takeover (n, adj)

take up (v)

takeup (n, adj)

talebearer

talemonger

taleteller

Taliban (takes singular verb)

tamperproof

tangible

tank (lowercase, even after a proper title—Leclerc tank)

tank car

tape deck

tape-record (v)

tape recorder

target, targetable, targeted, targeter, targeting

task force

taskmaster

tax collector

tax dodger

tax-exempt (um)

tax form

tax-free (um)

taxi(s)

taxpaying

tax-supported (um)

Tay-Sachs disease

teachers college

teammate

teamplay(er)

teamwork

tear down (v)

teardown (n, um)

tear gas (n, um)

teargas, teargassed (v)

teenage(er)

tele (cf, all one word)

  televise

telltale

tendency

tenfold

terminus, termini (pl)

terrible

territorywide

test bed

test-fire (v)

test-fly (v)

test-jamming (v)

test-launch (v)

test range

test site

test stand

tete-a-tete

textbook

thanksgiving
but Thanksgiving Day

thank-you (n)

theater

theatergoing

theaterwide

The Bahamas

The Gambia

The Hague

themselves

then (adj) **Premier**

    then second deputy minister

then-ruling (um)

then-troublesome (um)

thereafter

thereby

therefor (for it)

therefore (for that reason)

thereunder

thereupon

thesis, theses (pl)

thickheaded

thickskinned

think factory

think-piece

think tank

thinskinned

third-class (adj)

third-country (adj)

third-degree (adj)

thirdhand (adv, adj)

third-order (um)

third-party (adj)

third-quarter (adj)

third-rate (adj)

Third World countries

thirtysomething(s)

thoroughbred

thoroughfare

thoroughgoing

thought-provoking (um)

threat-driven (um)

three-dimensional (um)

threefold

threesome

threshold

throughout

throughput

through road

throughway

throw away (v)

throwaway (n, um)

throw back (v)

throwback (n, um)

throw line

throw rope

throw weight (n, um)

thumbnail

thunderclap

thunderhead

thundershower

thunderstorm

Tiananmen Square

ticketholder

ticket seller

tidal wave

tideland

tidetable

tidewater

tide-worn (um)

tiebreaker

tie in (v)

tie-in (n, um)

ties to

tie up (v)

tieup (n, um)

tightfisted

tightlipped

tightrope

tightwad

timberland

time (suffix, often solid)

    daytime

    halftime

    peacetime

    but

    full-time

    part-time

time being

time bomb

timeclock

time-consuming (um)

time-delay (um)

time frame

time-honored (um)

timekeeper

timekilling

timelag

timeline

time-out (n)

timepiece

timesaving

time-sensitive (um)

timeserver

time-share

time-sharing (comp)

timeslot

timespan

timetable

time-urgent (um)

timewasting

timeworn

tip off (v)

tipoff (n, um)

tiptoe

titleholder

title page

title-winning (um)

T-jetty

today

to-do (n)

toehold

toll bridge

tollgate

toll road

Tomahawk-class missile

tomorrow

tone-deaf (um)

toneup (n, um)

tongue-lash (v)

tongue lashing

tonguetied

tongue twister

tongue-twisting (um)

tonight

ton-kilometer

toolbuilding

toolfitter

toolkit

toolshop

toolsmith

tool steel

toolwork

toothache

tooth and nail

toothbrush

toothpaste

top brass

top drawer

topflight (adj)

topheavy

top-level (adj)

topline

topliner

topmost

topnotch

top-quality (adj)

top-secret (um)

topside (nautical)

topsy-turvy

torchlight

torpedo boat

torpedo mine

torpedo room

torpedo tube

torsion bar (n, um)

tortuous (adj, twisting, devious, highly complex)

torturous (adj, causing torture, cruelly painful)

tossup (n, um)

total, totaled, totaling

touch and go

touchdown (n, um)

touchup (n, um)

tough-minded (um)

toward

to wit

townhall

town meeting

townspeople

traceable

track-mobile (um)

tractor-trailer

tradeable

tradecraft

trade in (v)

trade-in (n, um)

trademark

trade name

trade-off (n, um)

trade off (v)

trade school

tradesperson, tradespeople

trade union

trade unionism

trade unionist

trade unions

trade wind

trafficking

trailblazing

trainborne

training camp

training ship

trainload

trainmaster

trainshed

train station

trainyard

tramcar

tramline

tramrail

tramway

tranquilize(r)

tranquillity

trans (pref)

    trans-Canadian

    trans-Siberian

    rest one word

    transalpine

    transatlantic

    transisthmian

    transonic

    transpacific

    transship

    transshipment

    transuranic

transcendent

transfer, transferred, transferring (*but* **transferable, transferal**)

transit, transited, transiting

transmit, transmitted, transmitting, transmittal, transmittance

transporter-erector-launcher (n)

trapdoor

travel, traveled, traveler, traveling

traveler's checks

traveltime

travel-worn (um)

treatybound

treatybreaking

treaty-limited

treatymaking

tree line

tree-lined (um)

tree-ripe (um)

treetop

tree trunk

tri (cf)

    tri-iodide

    tri-ply

    rest one word

    tricolor

    tripartite

    tristate

Trilateral Accords (Ukraine)

tribesman

tribespeople

trigger-happy (um)

triple-edged (um)

triple play

tripwire

Trojan horse

trolley bus

trolley car

trolley line

troopship

troop train

troop training (n, um)

trouble-free (um)

troublemaking

troubleshooter

troublesome

trouble spot

truckborne

truckdriver

truck farm

truckline

truckload

truckstop

truck tractor

truck trailer

true-blue (um)

trunkline

trust-building (um)

trust-busting (um)

try out (v)

tryout (n, um)

T-shaped

T-shirt

T-square

Tu-16 Badger

tube-feed, tube-fed (v)

tugboat

tug of war

tune up (v)

tuneup (n, um)

turbo (cf)

    turbo-ramjet

    rest one word

turn

    turn about (v)

    turnabout (n, um)

    turn around (v)

    turnaround (n, um)

    turn back (v)

    turnback (n, um)

    turncoat

    turn down (v)

    turndown (n, um)

    turn in (v)

    turn-in (n, um)

    turnkey

    turn off (v)

    turnoff (n, um)

    turn out (v)

    turnout (n, um)

    turn over (v)

    turnover (n, um)

    turnpike

    turnscrew

    turntable

turned-on (um)

turned-out (um)

turret deck

turret gun

turret ship

turtleback

20th-century (adj)

twenty-first

twenty-one

twentysomething(s)

twice-reviewed (um)

twin-engine (adj)

twin-engined (um)

twin-jet (adj)

twin-screw (adj)

two-faced (um)

twofold

two-piece (adj)

two-plus-four (German reunification talks)

two-seater

two-sided (um)

twosome

two-thirds

two-way (adj)

two-wheeler

typecast

typeface

typescript

typesetting

typewriting

ultra (pref)

    ultra-ambitious

    ultra-atomic

    ultra-English

    ultra-high-frequency (adj)

    ultra-high-speed (adj)

    ultra-high-voltage (adj)

    ultra-large-scale (adj)

    rest one word

    ultrahigh

    ultraorthodox

    ultrarightwing

    ultrashortwave

    ultrasonic

    ultraviolet

un (pref)

    un-American

    un-ionized

    uncalled-for (um)

    unheard-of (um)

    unMIRVed

    unself-conscious

    unsent-for (um)

    unthought-of (um)

    rest one word

    unaware (adj)

    unawares (adv)

UN Charter

under

    underage (n, deficit; um, too young)

    under age (pred)

    under contract

    undercover (um)

    undercoverman

    undercultivation (insufficient cultivation)

    under cultivation (being tilled)

    undercut

    underdog

undergo

underground (all senses)

under-ice (adj)

under oath

under obligation

under orders

underpriced

underside

under secretary, under secretaries

under-secretaryship

under strength (pred)

understrength (um)

under suspicion

under-the-counter (um)

under water (pred)

underwater (um)

under way (pred)

underway (um)

    as prefix, one word

uni (cf, usually one word)

UN-initiated (um)

unintelligible

uninterruptible power supple (comp)

union-made (um)

union shop

UN Mission

UN Permanent Representative

UN Special Commission (UNSCOM)

UN Special Representative

up

    up-and-comer (n)

    up-and-coming (um)

    upbeat

    upcountry

    update

    upend (v)

    up-front (um)

    upgrade

    uphill

upkeep

uplift

up-link

upload (comp)

uprange

upriver

upstairs

upstream

upswing

up time (comp)

up-to-date

uptown

upturn

upwind

uppercase (printing)

upper caste

upper-class (adj)

upperclassman

uppercrust (n, um)

upper hand

upper-house (adj)

upper-income (adj)

upper house, lower house (um, in Japanese context)

upper-middle-class (adj)

uppermost

UPS (comp, uninterruptible power supply)

URL (comp, Uniform Resource Locator)

US $3 million

usable

user friendly (comp)

userid (comp)

upside down

US-owned (um)

U-turn

value added (n, v)

value-added (um)

vaporware (comp)

VAR (comp, value-added reseller)

variable rate mortgage

V-E Day

Veteran's Day

very-high-frequency (adj)

very-low-frequency (adj)

vice

>vice admiral
>
>vice-admiralty
>
>vice chair
>
>vice chancellor
>
>vice consul
>
>vice-consulate
>
>vice-marshall
>
>vice-consulship
>
>vice minister
>
>vice-ministry
>
>vice-presidency
>
>vice president

vice-presidential

>vice-president-elect (general sense)
>
>*but* Vice President–elect

vice versa

videocassette

videoconferencing

videotape (n, v)

>*but* video tape recording

Vietnam war

viewpoint

vis-a-vis

voice activated

voice mail

Voice of America

volt-ampere

voltmeter

volt-second

vote-casting (um)

votegetter

vote-getting (um)

viewgraph (overhead, transparency)

VRAM (comp, video RAM)

VRML (comp, Virtual Reality Modeling Language)

wage earner

wage-earning (um)

wage scale

wagonload

wait-and-see (adj)

waiting list

waiting period

wake-homing

walkie-talkie

walk in (v)

walk-in (n, um)

walk on (v)

walk-on (n, um)

walk out (v)

walkout (n, um)

walled-in (um)

walled-up (um)

wall-like

wallpaper

WAN (comp, wide-area network)

war

    war chest (n)

    war-crimes (um)

    warfighter

    warfighting (n)

    war-fighting (um)

    war game (n)

    war-game (v, adj)

    wargaming (n)

    warhead

    warhorse (nonliteral)

    warlike

    warlord

    warmaking

    warmonger

    warpath

    warplanes

    warplans

    warship

    wartime

war-torn

war-waging (um)

war-wearied (um)

war weariness

war-weary (um)

war-winning (um)

ward (suffix, usually one word)

    afterward

    homeward

    northward

wardheeler

wardrobe

warehouse

warmed-over (um)

warm up (v)

warmup (n, um)

Warsaw Pact Treaty

washed-out

wash out (v)

washout (n, um)

wash up (v)

washup (n, um)

Wassenaar Agreement

wastewater

watchband

watchdog

watch list

watchman

watchword

water-bearing (um)

water body

waterborne

watercolor

water-cool (v)

water-cooled (um)

water-cut (from oil well)

watered-down (um)

waterfall

water-filled (um)

waterflood (of oil wells)

waterflow

waterfront

waterhole

water level

waterline

waterlogged

water main

waterman

watermark (as on stationery)

    but high water mark (as in floods)

waterpower

waterproof

water sharing (n)

water-sharing (um)

watershed

waterside

waterski

water-soaked (um)

water-soluble (um)

water table

watertight

water tower

water treatment (um)

waterway

waterworks

watthour (Wh)

wave band

waveform

wave front

waveguide

wave height

wavelength

wave-swept (um)

way station

weak-kneed (um)

weaponmaking

weapons-grade

weapons of mass destruction (WMD)

weapons-of-mass-destruction (um)

weapons-related (um)

weapon system (preferred), weapons system

weatherbeaten

weather-hardened (um)

weather map

weatherproof

weatherstrip

Web browser (comp)

Web site (comp)

weekday

weekend

weekender

weeklong (adj)

week-old (adj)

well-being (n)

well-born (um)

well-bred (um)

well-coordinated (um)

well-doer

well-done (um)

well-drilling (um)

well field

wellhead

wellhouse

well-informed (um)

well-known (um)

well-looking (um)

well-off (um)

well-prepared (um)

well-read (um)

well-spoken (um)

wellspring

well-thought-of (um)

well-thought-out (um)

well-to-do

well-trained (um)

well-wisher

well-worn (um)

westbound

west-central

west end

Western European Union (WEU)

Western-government-backed (um)

Western Hemisphere

westernmost

westmost

west-northwest

westward

wet (of water)

wetland

wheatfield

wheatgrower

wheatland

wheat-rich (um)

wheatstalk

wheelbarrow

wheelbase

wheelbox

wheelchair

wheeler-dealer

wheelpower

whereabouts

whereas

whereby

whereupon

wherever

wherewithal

whet (to stimulate)

whichever

whipcord

whip hand

whiplash

whirlpool

whistle-blower, whistle-blowing

whistlestop

white book (diplomatic)

whitecap (nonliteral)

white-collar (adj, nonliteral)

white count

white flag

white goods

white lie

white paper (diplomatic)

whitewash

whoever

wholehearted

wholesale

wholesome

wholly owned subsidiary

wide (suffix, usually unhyphenated)

    armywide

    nationwide

    peninsulawide

    but

    Africa-wide

    Army-wide

wide-angle (adj)

wide-area (adj)

wide-awake (adj)

wide-band (adj)

wide-body (n, adj)

wide gauge (n)

wide-gauge (um)

wide-open (um)

wide-ranging (um)

wide-scale (adj)

widespread

widthwise

wild card

wildflower

wildlife

willful

willpower

willy-nilly

wind

    windblown

    windborne

    windbreak

    windburn

    windchill

windfall

windmill

windpipe

windpower

windproof

windshield

windspeed

windstorm

windswept

wind-tunnel (um)

windward

window-dressing

windowsill

wind up (v)

windup (n, um)

wine-making (um)

wing flap

wingspan

wingspread

wingtip

winter (season)

winterkill

winterproof

winter-sown (um)

wintertime

winter wheat

wireline

wirephoto

wiretap

wise (suffix, usually one word)

    businesswise

    clockwise

wisecrack

wise guy

wise man

wise-spoken (um)

wish list

wishy-washy

witch hunt

withdraw

withhold

within

without

withstand

WMD (weapons of mass destruction)

woodland

woodpulp

woodwork

woolgathering

wool-lined (um)

woolshearing

woolworking

wordbook

wordbuilding

word combination

wordcraft

word-for-word (adj, adv)

wordlist

word-of-mouth (adj, adv)

wordplay

word watcher

word wrap (comp)

work

    workday

    workflow

    work force

    workhorse

    work hour

    workload

    workman

    workmanlike

    workmanship

    work order

    workout

    workplace

    workplan

    worksaving

    worksheet

    work shift

    workshop

    worksite

    workspace

workstation

workteams

worktime

workup

workweek

workyard

workyear

working-class (adj)

working day

working-level (adj)

workingman

workingwoman

worldbeater

world-class (adj)

World Court

worldview

World War II period

worldwide

World Wide Web (comp, **WWW**)

WORM (comp, write-once, read-many)

wornout (um)

worrywart

worship, worshiped, worshiper, worshiping

worst case (n, um)

worthwhile

would-be

wrack (wreck)

wrap up (v)

wrap-up (n, um)

wreak (to cause)

write down (v)

write-down (n, adj)

write in (v)

write-in (n, um)

write off (v)

writeoff (n, um)

write protected (comp)

writers guide

write up (v)

writeup (n, um)

wrongdoer

wrong-minded (um)

wrong-thinking (um)

wrought iron

WWW (comp, **World Wide Web**)

Wye River Memorandum (*but* Wye accord)

xerox (use **photocopy** unless trade name Xerox)
X-ray
X-shaped

Yak-40

yearbook

yearend

yearlong

year-old

year on year (adv)

year-on-year (um)

year-round

years' (possessive case)

yellowcake (of uranium)

yellow fever

Yel'tsin

yes-man

yesterday

yet-determined (um)

yet-to-be

Y-joint

young-looking (um)

Young Turk(s)

yourself

youthlike

zero-gravity (um)

zero(s)

zero-sum (um)

zigzag

Index

incredible, 59
incredulous, 59
incumbent
    titles of persons, 108
indefinite articles, 59
indefinite numbers, 72
indicate, 60
indigenous, 41
individual, 60
INF, 101
infinitives, 60
    titles of publications, 111
inflammable, 49
injuries, 60
in order to, 60
installations
    proper names, 91
insure, 12, 46, 61
intensify, 46
interestingly, 58
in terms of, 61
international organizations
    titles of persons, 110
introductory clause
    commas, 23
-ise, 45
italics, 61
    art, 61
    crafts, 61
    foreign titles of publications, 112
    foreign words, 50
    quotation marks, 95
    titles, 61
    titles of publications, 111
-ize, 45

J
joint, 21
Jr., 24
judicial branch
    titles of persons, 109

K
kind, 114
known as, 95

L
lack, 63
lasting, 123
Latin, 63

Latin abbreviations, 63
latter, 63
laws
    capitalization, 113
    references, 41
legislative bills
    references, 41
legislative branch
    titles of persons, 109
less, 49
letter or number elements, 63
letter-number combinations, 73
    plurals, 11
letters
    cross-references, 31
    designators, 37
    footnote references, 49
    hyphens, 29
    indefinite articles, 59, 60
    parentheses, 81
    plural designators, 39
    plurals, 11
like, 64, 113
likely, 64
likewise, 64
linguistic
    capitalization, 69
links, 99
-ly, 45, 116

M
m², 73
Mach units
    units of measure, 117
majority, 65, 83
margin, 65
may, 30
MBFR, 101
media, 33
mercifully, 58
metric system
    units of measure, 117
Metropolitan
    geographic terms, 54
mid-, 25
might, 30
migrate, 44
military, 65
    coined names, 19
    titles of persons, 110

www.ingramcontent.com/pod-product-compliance
Lightning Source LLC
Chambersburg PA
CBHW082352270326
41935CB00013B/1594

9 781931 641029